The Biologic
Economic B(

A Concise Introduct

David McFarland

Emeritus Fellow, Balliol College, University of Oxford, UK

palgrave
macmillan

First published 2016 by
PALGRAVE MACMILLAN

Palgrave Macmillan in the UK is an imprint of Macmillan Publishers Limited, registered in England, company number 785998, of Houndmills, Basingstoke, Hampshire RG21 6XS.

Palgrave Macmillan in the US is a division of St Martin's Press LLC, 175 Fifth Avenue, New York, NY 10010.

Palgrave Macmillan is the global academic imprint of the above companies and has companies and representatives throughout the world.

Palgrave® and Macmillan® are registered trademarks in the United States, the United Kingdom, Europe and other countries.

ISBN 978-1-137-56808-3

This book is printed on paper suitable for recycling and made from fully managed and sustained forest sources. Logging, pulping and manufacturing processes are expected to conform to the environmental regulations of the country of origin.

A catalogue record for this book is available from the British Library.

Library of Congress Cataloging-in-Publication Data
McFarland, David, author.
  The biological bases of economic behaviour : a concise introduction /
  David McFarland.
    pages   cm
  Includes bibliographical references.
  ISBN 978–1–137–56808–3 (pbk. : alk. paper)
  1. Animal behavior—Economic aspects.   2. Decision making in animals.
  3. Evolution (Biology)   4. Economics—Psychological aspects.
  5. Economic anthropology.   6. Psychology, Comparative.   I. Title.
  QL785.M455 2016
  591.5—dc23   2015025772

The Biological Bases of Economic Behaviour

Contents

Figures

Preface

This book is firmly aimed at students of economics. It offers an opportunity to think about microeconomics from a biological viewpoint. Biologists may well be dissatisfied by the level of explanation, but we have in mind that economics students, on the whole, have relatively little biological background. Economists may well be dissatisfied with the level of economic detail, but we are assuming that economics students will be getting that anyway.

Economics students do not have to defend any particular viewpoint. Given time, they can choose their own particular viewpoint. All we hope to do in this book is to stimulate some thought along biological lines.

The first Nobel Prize for Economics was awarded to Ragnar Frisch and Jan Tinbergen in 1969. Jan Tinbergen's brother, Niko Tinbergen, was awarded the Nobel Prize for Medicine, together with Karl von Frisch and Konrad Lorenz in 1973.

Niko Tinbergen believed that the behaviour of any animal could only be properly understood in terms of four questions (causation, development, function, and evolution). Humans are animals, and it seems to be an irony of history that Tinbergen's four questions are not asked, or addressed by economists, in relation to the economic behaviour of humans. One would hope that behavioural economists, at least, would have some grasp of these essentials, but it seems to us that there has been little progress since John Maynard Keynes, in 1936, conjured up "animal spirits" to account for the apparently aberrant behaviour of economic man. I thank my friend Tom Bosser for encouraging me to start this book, and I thank my wife, Penelope, for putting up with the consequences.

1
The Evolution of Economic Behaviour

The biological bases of economics include all those biological
factors that influence the economic behaviour of individual animals.
Humans are animals, and another way of addressing the subject is
to ask – what are the fundamental biological factors that influence
microeconomic behaviour? We need to start with some fundamental
biological concepts, because human behaviour, including economic
behaviour, is the product of evolutionary pressures that are the result
of **natural selection**, whether they be cultural or genetic. Any student of economic behaviour should consider whether, and to what
extent, such influences are important, because it is possible that the
homunculus within current economic theory may be too simple, and
not truly representative of the behaviour of ordinary people. In this
book we will be exploring an array of biological phenomena, and
inviting the student of economics to consider to what extent they
are relevant to the modern economic situation.

Evolution by natural selection

Biological evolution is the development of species' characteristics
from earlier forms, now acknowledged to be due to the process of
natural selection. Animal behaviour can only be fully understood in
terms of its evolutionary history, and in terms of the role that it plays
in survival and reproduction (more precisely, the **inclusive fitness** of
the animal).

Evolutionary biologists are interested in explaining how a state
of affairs observed today (such as the behaviour typical of a certain

species) is likely to have come about as a result of evolution by natural selection. To account for the establishment of a particular genetic trait, they imagine a time before the trait existed. Then they postulate that a rare gene arises in an individual, or arises with an immigrant, and that individuals carrying the gene exhibit the trait. They then ask what circumstances will favour the spread of the gene through the population. If a gene is favoured by natural selection, then individuals with genotypes incorporating the gene will have increased fitness. The gene may be said to have invaded the population. To become established a gene must not only compete with the existing members of the gene pool, but must also resist invasion by other mutant genes. It is as if genes develop a strategy to increase their numbers at the expense of other genes. Thus an **evolutionary strategy** is a passive result of natural selection that gives the appearance of a ploy employed by genes to increase their numbers at the expense of other genes. So an evolutionary strategy is not a strategy in the cognitive sense, but a theoretical tool employed by evolutionary biologists.

Life history strategy

Individual animals are born, enjoy a particular lifestyle, and then die. The characteristic lifestyle of a given species is the subject of life-history theory. This body of theory asserts that natural selection shapes the timing and duration of key events of an organism's life to produce the greatest possible number of surviving offspring.

The most important events include juvenile development, the age of sexual maturity, the timing of reproductive events, the number and size of offspring, the level of parental investment, and the lifespan that is typical of the species. For a given individual, the resources that can be allocated to these events are finite. The time and energy devoted to one event diminishes the time and energy available for the others.

Of prime importance is the notion of **reproductive value**, the expected contribution to the population by current and future reproduction. Animal species that live in unpredictable or unstable environments usually reproduce quickly (i.e. have a short generation period). There is little advantage in adaptations that permit competition with other animals, since the environment is likely to change. They tend to invest in numerous, inexpensive offspring that disperse widely. For species that inhabit stable and predictable environments competition with other animals is an important factor. Such species tend to have a long generation period and few well-cared-for offspring. Examples include elephants, whales, and humans. The majority of animals fall between these two extremes. Indeed we can look at the situation as a life-history spectrum. The implication of this line of thinking is that it is in the nature of individual humans (i.e. their characteristic **life-history strategy**) to care not only for their personal lifestyle, but also for that of their offspring and relatives. You may think this a bit far-fetched, but consider the following.

The experimental physiologist Michel Cabanac (a name to remember) asked his subjects (students) to adopt a certain posture and to hold this posture for as long as they could. It was a sitting posture, back against a wall but with nothing to sit on. After a short while holding this posture becomes painful. In a series of experiments Cabanac paid the subjects differing amounts (per session) per second for holding the posture for as long as they could. He found that, within limits, the greater the rate of pay, the longer the subjects would hold the painful posture. This experiment was repeated in Oxford, but with a difference. In some sessions, the money went, not to the subject, but to a named relative of the subject. In other words, the subject was told before the session that today the money would be sent to their aunt, or cousin, and so on. The subjects had previously been asked for details of their relatives. The amounts of money sent out were rather small, usually about £1. The experiment was then repeated in London, and in South Africa where the subjects were Zulus from both urban and rural backgrounds (in the latter case the payment was made in food).[1] In all cases it was found that the subjects would hold the posture for longer the more closely related (in terms of their **coefficient of relatedness**) they were to the recipients of the money/food. In other words, the subjects were putting up with pain, not for their own benefit, but for that of a relative. Apart from the biological implications of these results (see below) there are economic implications. They suggest that a person's economic aspirations are likely to include benefits to relatives, albeit implicitly.

Kith and kin

It is a biological imperative for parents to be able to identify their offspring. For example, amongst a flock of sheep, when the young lambs gather together in play, there is a danger that a mother may have her milk taken by a lamb that is not hers. She identifies her offspring by smell, turning around to check whoever is suckling. To permit another's lamb to suckle would be a form of **altruism.**

Altruistic behaviour benefits other animals at some cost to the donor. In evolutionary biology, altruism is defined by reference to its effects on survival prospects without reference to any motivation or intention that may be involved. The possibility that animals may have altruistic or selfish intentions is, of course, of interest, but it is not relevant to consideration of altruism from an evolutionary point of view. This distinction is sometimes forgotten.

As we have seen, the age at which an animal should ideally become sexually mature and capable of reproduction is a matter of evolutionary life-history strategy. In unpredictable environments natural selection usually favours early maturity and large numbers of offspring which are left to fend for themselves. In more stable environments it is a better strategy to mature late and have few offspring which are well cared for. In general, the more time and energy a parent expends upon a particular offspring, the fitter that offspring will be. There is often an inverse relationship between the total number of offspring produced and their average fitness. An animal's individual fitness is a measure of its ability to leave viable offspring. The process of natural selection determines which characteristics of the animal confer greater fitness. However, the effectiveness of natural selection depends upon the mixture of genotypes in the population. Thus, the relative fitness of a genotype depends upon the other genotypes present in the population, as well as upon other environmental conditions.

The concept of fitness can be applied to individual genes by considering the survival of particular genes in the gene pool from one generation to another. A gene that can enhance the reproductive success of the animal carrying it will thereby increase its representation in the gene pool. It could do this by influencing the animal's morphology or physiology, making it more likely to survive climatic and other hazards, or by influencing its behaviour, making the animal more successful in courtship or raising young. A gene that influences parental behaviour will probably be represented in the offspring so that by facilitating parental care, the gene itself is likely to appear in other individuals. Indeed, a situation could arise in which the gene could have a deleterious effect upon the animal carrying it but increase its probability of survival in the offspring. An obvious example is a gene that leads the parent to endanger its own life in attempts to preserve the lives of its progeny. This is a form of altruism.

By the mid 20th century, biologists had realized that the fitness of an individual gene could be increased as a result of altruistic behaviour on the part of animals carrying the gene. However, William Hamilton (1964) was the first to enunciate the general principle that natural selection tends to maximize not individual fitness but inclusive fitness; that is, an animal's fitness depends upon not only its own reproductive success but also that of its kin. The inclusive fitness of an individual depends upon the survival of its descendants and of its collateral relatives. Thus even if an animal has no offspring its inclusive fitness may not be zero, because its genes will be passed on by nieces, nephews, and cousins.[2]

Reciprocal altruism

Altruism towards kin can be regarded as selfishness on the part of the genes responsible, because copies of these genes are likely to be present in relatives. Altruism could also be regarded as a form of gene selfishness if by being altruistic an individual could ensure that it was a recipient of altruism at a later date. The problem with the evolution of this reciprocal kind of altruism is that individuals that cheated, by receiving but never giving, would be at an advantage.

It is possible that cheating could be countered if individuals were altruistic only toward other individuals that were likely to reciprocate. For example, when a female olive baboon (*Papio anubis*) comes into oestrus, a male forms a consort relationship with her. He follows her around, waiting for an opportunity to mate, and guards the female from the attentions of other males. However, a rival male may sometimes solicit the help of a third male in an attempt to gain access to the female. While the solicited male challenges the consort male to a fight, the rival male gains access to the female. The altruism shown by the solicited male is often reciprocated. Those males that most often gave aid were those that most frequently received such aid.[3]

This type of **reciprocal altruism** obviously provides scope for cheating. An individual that receives aid may refuse to reciprocate at a later date. However, if opportunities for reciprocal altruism arise sufficiently often, and if the individuals involved are known to each other, then a non-cooperative individual can be identified easily and discriminated against. Thus, for natural selection to favour reciprocal altruism, the individuals must have sufficient opportunities for reciprocation, they must be able to recognize each other individually and remember their obligations, and they must be motivated to reciprocate. These conditions are found in primitive human societies, and reciprocal altruism has played an important role in human evolution.[4]

Cultural evolution

Evolution occurs as a result of natural selection, and inheritance of acquired characteristics is not normally possible. However, much an individual animal adapts to its environment, whether by learning or by physiological adaptation, the acquired adaptations cannot be passed to the offspring by genetic means. So much is widely accepted among biologists. However, information can be passed from parent to offspring by **imitation** and by **imprinting**. In general, the passage of information from one generation to the next by non-genetic means is known as cultural exchange.

Sensitive periods of learning occur in the early life of many animals. During such periods they often learn from their parents. For example, the white crowned sparrow will remember its parents' song provided it hears it during the sensitive period between 10 and 50 days old. Individuals prevented from hearing the song of their own species during this period never produce a proper white crowned sparrow song during later life. Whereas the juvenile white crowned sparrow will not learn songs that are much different from the song of its own species, other birds, such as the bullfinch, will learn the song of a completely different species. Thus a juvenile bullfinch fostered by a canary will adopt canary song. The tendency to copy the song of the parents leads to regional variations even among species that will learn only songs similar to that of their own species. In the region of San Francisco, for example, populations of white crowned sparrows separated by only a few miles have distinct dialects.[5]

Animal dialects represent an elementary form of tradition. Juvenile white crowned sparrows are inevitably exposed to the song dialect characteristic of the locality in which they are born, because their sensitive period of learning occurs before they are mobile. Other forms of traditional behaviour include the migration routes of some mammals and birds. Geese, ducks, and swans migrate in flocks composed of mixed juveniles and adults. The juveniles learn the route that is characteristic of their population, stopping at traditional rest places and breeding and over-wintering localities.[6] There are many other examples. Reindeer also show fidelity to traditional migration routes and calving grounds. Migratory salmon hatch in freshwater streams and migrate to the sea. The juveniles become imprinted on the odour of their native stream and return to the same stream as adults to spawn in the traditional places. Some game trails of deer and other mammals are known to have been used for centuries. In parts of Britain and Germany, where roads have been built across the traditional migratory routes of toads, conservationists stand guard during the breeding season to prevent the toads from being run over by motorists.

Simple forms of traditional behaviour do not require any special learning abilities, or any special teaching. They arise as an inevitable consequence of the circumstances in which the young are raised and of the tendency of juvenile animals to become imprinted upon their habitat, their parents, and their peers. In some animals, however, more complex forms of learning are involved. For example, tool use in primates can spread through a population, as a result of imitative learning.

Imitation is not always what it seems. Animals may copy each other as a result of simple **social facilitation**. Many animals eat more when fed in groups than when fed alone. This has been demonstrated experimentally in chickens, puppies, fish, and opossums. If a chicken is allowed to eat until completely satiated, and is then introduced to others that are still feeding, the satiated bird will resume eating. Domestic chicks also have a tendency to peck when others peck, even if there is no food available. Chicks tend to peck at the same type of food-like particle as the mother hen. The tendency to concentrate on the type of food being eaten by others has also been demonstrated in sparrows and chaffinches.[7]

Avoidance of noxious food can also be socially facilitated. Attempts to kill large flocks of the common crow in the United States, by providing poisoned bait, were not successful because the majority avoided the bait after a few individuals had been poisoned. Similarly, the reaction of just one rat to novel food may be sufficient to determine the reactions of other rats in the group. If one rat eats the food, then others will join in, but if that rat sniffs the food and rejects it, the others will reject it. Sometimes, the pioneer rat urinates on the bait, thus warning others to reject it.[8] Social attraction to, and avoidance of, food often result from a tendency to investigate places where other members of the species have been observed, rather than direct copying of the behaviour of others. This is probably the case with the tradition of stealing milk by blue tits in England. For many years milk was delivered to houses in England and left on the doorstep early in the morning. Blue tits, and sometimes great tits, pecked through the foil tops of the bottles and helped themselves to the rich cream that floats on the top of the milk. This practice first appeared in particular localities and gradually spread, suggesting that the birds were learning from each other.[9]

From these examples it is obvious that culture and tradition do not require great intelligence on the part of individuals. Although highly developed culture and highly developed intelligence are both primarily human traits, they are not necessarily causally related. There are many cultural practices found in primitive human societies that are biologically adaptive, but not obviously the result of reasoning. For example, most of the traditional methods of cooking maize (corn) by the indigenous people of the New World involve some kind of alkali treatment. Often the maize is boiled for about 40 minutes in water containing wood ash, lye, or dissolved lime. It is then eaten directly, or converted into dough, tortillas, and so on. The alkali treatment is practised for purely traditional reasons, although it may be said by some to make the food more palatable. However, the alkali treatment has important nutritional consequences. The local maize has low levels of available lysine, a nutritionally essential amino acid. Most of the lysine in maize occurs as part of an indigestible protein. The alkali treatment breaks up the protein, and greatly improves the nutritional quality of the food. Some kind of alkali treatment is found in all indigenous cultures that rely on maize, and it is probable that natural selection, acting through malnutrition, has eliminated those people who did not follow the traditional practice.

Thus we see that although culture can short-circuit biological heredity, and lead to very rapid evolution, the products of cultural evolution are still subject to natural selection. Although some learning ability is essential for cultural change, no great intelligence is necessary, and those people who follow traditional practices are often unable to give a rational explanation of their behaviour. However, humans also evolved some traits that predisposed them towards rapid cultural evolution. These are tool using, language, and writing.

Tool use and intelligence

The ability to use tools has long been regarded as an aspect of intelligence, and the ability to make tools once was regarded as a factor that set humans apart from other animals. Now that we know much more about tool using in animals, the issue is not so clear-cut, although the manufacture of tools is regarded widely as an important influence upon human evolution.

Tool use can be defined as the use of an external object as a functional extension of the body to attain an immediate goal.[10] This definition excludes some cases of manipulation of objects by animals and includes others. Crows take whelks up into the air and drop them on a rock to break them open. Other birds have similar behaviour. Thus song thrushes (*Turdus philomelos*) hold snails in their beak and smash them against a rock anvil, while ravens (*Corvus corax*) and some vultures (*Gypaetus barbatus*) drop bones in order to crack them open to feed on the marrow. The use of a stone anvil to break open food items, however, does not count as tool using because the anvil is not an extension of the animal's body.

The Egyptian vulture (*Neophron percnopterus*) is known to break ostrich eggs by throwing them against a stone anvil. This does not count as tool using. However, the vultures also may carry a stone into the air and drop it onto an ostrich nest or pick up a stone in the beak and throw it at an egg. These uses of a stone do count as tool use because the stone can be regarded as an extension of the vulture's body.

An animal that scratches or rubs itself against a tree is not using the tree as a tool, but an elephant or horse that picks up a stick to scratch itself is using the stick as an extension of its body for a short-term purpose. However, a bird that carries twigs to build a nest is using the twig as material and not as an extension of its body. A nest is not normally regarded as a tool for raising the young because it achieves a long-term rather than a short-term objective.

The Galapagos woodpecker finch (*Cactospiza pallida*) probes for insects in crevices in the bark of trees by holding a cactus spine in its beak. This clearly counts as tool using by the earlier definition, but should it count as a sign of intelligence? From the functional point of view, the use of a cactus spine to probe for food is an intelligent solution to a particular problem. A human who hit upon this solution to the problem would normally be regarded as showing signs of intelligence. Those who wish to judge intelligence purely on the basis of appropriate responses to circumstances have to allow that the finch is behaving intelligently.

If the behaviour of the woodpecker finch were largely innate, then we probably would not want to count its probing behaviour as intelligent. Observations of a juvenile woodpecker finch that had been taken from the nest as a fledgling[11] show that the bird manipulated twigs from an early age. If the hungry bird was presented with an insect in a hole, it would drop the twig and try to obtain the insect with its beak. Gradually, the bird began to probe for insects with a twig, and it seems likely that learning plays some part in the development of the behaviour. Does this make us more inclined to regard the behaviour as an indication of intelligence? We have to be very careful here. Even if it is true that learning plays a part in the development of the behaviour, it seems likely that woodpecker finches are predisposed genetically to learn this particular type of manipulation in much the same way that some birds are predisposed to learn particular types of song. Conversely, the probing behaviour is the functional equivalent of intelligent behaviour, and we must resist the temptation to say that the bird is not really intelligent just because it is a bird and not a mammal. We must be careful to use the same criteria in judging the bird's behaviour as we would in judging similar behaviour in a chimpanzee.

Chimpanzees in the wild have been observed to make use of sticks, twigs, and grass stems to probe for food items. Grass stems may be used to probe for termites. These are chosen with care and may be modified to make them more suitable for their purpose. For example, if the end becomes bent, the chimps may bite it off.[12] Juvenile chimps may manipulate grass stems during play, but they do not use them for probing for food until they are about three years old. Even then they are often clumsy and may select tools that are not appropriate for the task. The skill required in probing for termites does not appear to be learned easily. Wild chimpanzees have also been observed to use sticks to obtain honey from bees' nests and to dig up plants with edible roots. They may use leaves as a sponge to obtain drinking water from a hole in a tree or to clean various parts of the body. Although tool use has been studied most intensively in wild chimpanzees, it has also been observed in other wild primates. Thus, baboons may use stones to squash scorpions and twigs to probe for insects.[13] The ability to use tools in natural situations probably develops in the individual through a mixture of imitative and instrumental learning. In these respects tool using in primates is difficult to separate from the development of probing behaviour in the woodpecker finch. Some biologists, while admitting that tool using is not in itself a sign of intelligence, argue that it sets the stage for truly intelligent behaviour that involves innovation.

That innovations do occur among chimpanzees probing for termites is suggested by comparison of the methods used by different chimpanzee populations. Chimpanzees at Gombe, in East Africa, use twigs without previously peeling off the bark. They may use each end of the twig to probe in turn. Chimps at Okorobiko, in Central Africa, usually peel the bark off a twig before using it as a probe, and they use only one end. Chimpanzees from Mount Assirik in Senegal, West Africa, do not use twigs as a probe but instead use relatively large sticks to make holes in the termite mound through which they pick out the termites by hand.[14] These differences suggest that a certain amount of variation exists within a population that may lead to innovations that suit local circumstances. The technique of fishing for termites is learned by imitation and is passed through the population by cultural tradition.

That some aspects of behaviour that are typical of a certain population are maintained by cultural means is well documented.[15] In a few cases, inventions have been observed and their spread through the population recorded. A celebrated case concerns the Japanese macaques (*Macaca fuscata*) of Koshima Island.[16] To bring the monkeys into the open where they could be observed more readily, scientists supplemented their diet by scattering sweet potatoes on the beach. A 16-month-old female, called Imo, was observed to wash the sand off her potatoes in a stream. She continued this practice on a regular basis and soon was imitated by other monkeys, particularly those of her own age. Within 10 years, the habit had been acquired by the majority of the population, with the exception of adults more than 12 years old and infants of less than a year. Two years later Imo invented another food-cleaning procedure. Scientists had been scattering grain on the beach, and the monkeys picked grains up one at a time. Imo gathered handfuls of mixed sand and grain and threw them into the sea. The sand sank and the grain was scooped easily from the water surface. The new procedure spread through the population in a manner similar to that of potato washing. The new behaviour was adopted first by monkeys of Imo's own age. Mothers learned from juveniles and adult males were the last to catch on.

Was Imo an especially intelligent monkey? Imo made her discoveries by chance and learned to exploit them. She did not necessarily have any special insight into the situation. On the other hand, many human inventions came about in a similar way. If the invention leads to a genuine improvement in the monkeys' circumstances, it counts as a form of adaptive behaviour arrived at through the efforts of a single individual. As judged by the results, Imo appears to be highly intelligent, but if we require that intelligence involves certain mechanisms like reasoning, then we need to know more about Imo's thought processes before we make a judgement.

As for humans, simple stone tools, made by various species of *Homo*, date back more than two million years. More sophisticated tools made by *Homo neanderthalensis*, started to appear about 300,000 years ago. They made tools from stone, bone, and antlers, but these changed little from generation to generation. By contrast, tools made by *Homo sapiens* became increasingly sophisticated over the same period. These included bone needles, fish hooks, and buttons.

Human evolution

Humans (i.e. members of the genus *Homo*) have been on this planet for more than three million years. Of the dozen species identified so far, all are extinct apart from *Homo sapiens*. Humans are characterized by large brains and the ability to use stone tools. Note, however, that some other species have large brains (e.g. dolphins), and many other species use tools of one sort or another, as we have seen.

Homo sapiens has been around for more than a million years. They originated in Africa and repeatedly left Africa to populate Eurasia and the rest of the world. There is some evidence that they interbred with other human species during this period. Until about 12,000 years ago all humans lived as hunters and gatherers. Up to 1500 AD hunter-gatherers occupied a third of the earth, including the whole of

Australia, most of North America, and large parts of South America, Africa, and Asia.[17] So from an evolutionary viewpoint, we would expect humans to be genetically predisposed to a hunter-gatherer lifestyle, and to have an economic outlook that is appropriate to that lifestyle. However, there may have been some genetic changes during the past 12,000 years, and there has been a considerable amount of cultural evolution. So we should now consider to what extent these factors might have influenced modern human nature.

Recent genetic changes

Some genetic changes have been well documented. Primarily, these have to do with changes in response to climate and altitude, and in diet. This is not surprising, considering that waves of humans were dispersing out of Africa into other, very different, parts of the world.

Dark hair and skin give protection from the ultraviolet component of sunlight; however, anthropologist Peter Frost[18] notes that while most human populations have only one hair colour and one eye colour, Europeans are the exception. Their hair is black but also brown, flaxen, golden, or red; their eyes are brown but also blue, grey, hazel, or green. This diversity has its maximum in northern and eastern Europe. He asks "Why this colour diversity? And why only in Europe?"

There are three possibilities to consider. Firstly, in northern latitudes a fairer skin might be favoured by natural selection because the synthesis of vitamin D in the skin will be facilitated. Some research shows that dark-skinned people living in temperate climates have lower vitamin D levels than fair-skinned people, because melanin in the skin hinders vitamin D synthesis.[19] However, this theory would not explain the European diversity in hair and eye colour. Secondly, there may have been interbreeding with Neanderthals. Perhaps there was some gene flow between the two groups, but certainly not enough to account for the large number of Europeans with neither black hair nor brown eyes.[20] Thirdly, there may have been **sexual selection**.[21] This type of selection intensifies when males outnumber females among individuals ready to mate, or vice versa. Where one sex is in excess they will have to compete for mates, and unusual eye or hair colour may become attractive to members of the opposite sex.

As human populations spread out of Africa into new areas of the globe, they encountered a whole range of climatic and biological conditions. For example, those that moved north entered the reindeer habitat. Reindeer are indigenous to northern Eurasia, and North America (where they are known as Caribou), a land that was covered by ice during the last glacial period. Reindeer were once found as far south as Nevada and Tennessee in North America and Spain in Europe, but the ice started to recede about 12,000 years ago. Today, wild reindeer have disappeared from many areas, especially from the southern parts. Large populations of wild reindeer are still found in Siberia, Greenland, Alaska, and Canada. The last remaining wild reindeer in Europe are found in portions of southern Norway. Domesticated reindeer are mostly found in northern Scandinavia, Russia, and Iceland. The southern boundary of the species' natural range is approximately at 62° north latitude, though this may change as a result of global warming.

The great value of this species lies in its exploitation of the tundra. Reindeer are ruminants, eating mainly lichens in winter, especially "reindeer moss". However, they also eat the leaves of willows and birches, as well as sedges and grasses. Reindeer hunting by humans has a very long history and it is probable that humans started hunting reindeer in the Mesolithic and Neolithic periods. Norway and Greenland have unbroken traditions of hunting wild reindeer from the ice age until the present day. In the non-forested mountains of central Norway, it is still possible to find remains of stone built trapping pits and guiding walls built especially for hunting reindeer, probably during the Stone Age. Wild caribou are still hunted by the indigenous people of North America and Greenland.

Reindeer have been herded for centuries by several Arctic and sub-Arctic people including the Sami (Lapps). They are raised for their meat, hides, antlers, and also for milk and transportation. Reindeer are not considered fully domesticated, as they generally roam free on pasture grounds. In traditional nomadic herding reindeer herders migrate with their herds between coast and inland areas according to an annual migration route and herds are keenly tended. However, reindeer have never been bred in captivity, though they have long been tamed for milking as well as for use as draught animals and beasts of burden.

The indigenous peoples of North America, such as the Inuit (Eskimos) hunted caribou, but did not herd tame them for milking. Even faced with the same species in a similar environment as North Eurasian peoples, they did not bring these animals into semi-domestication. As we shall see, this difference is probably due to genetic differences between these two peoples of differing origin. Thus whereas the Inuit diet is composed of marine mammals, fish, caribou, small game, birds, and plants, the Sami depend on herded reindeer for milk and meat, and on fishing, gathering plants, and hunting small game and birds.

The normal mammalian condition is for the young of a species to exhibit reduced production of the enzyme lactase at the end of the weaning period. In non-dairy-consuming human societies, lactase production usually drops by about 90% during the first four years of life. People lacking lactase cannot digest milk. However, certain human populations have an inherited mutation[22] that results in a bypass of the shutdown in lactase production, making it possible for members of these populations to continue consuming fresh milk and other dairy products throughout their lives. If your remote ancestors were pastoralists, keeping cattle and goats, then you are likely to be lactose-tolerant and able to digest milk as an adult. Scientists believe that Northern Europeans and certain African tribes evolved lactose tolerance independently, whereas people of Mongolian descent do not have the genetic makeup that enables them to digest milk as adults.[23] As we have seen, reindeer herders of North America have no milk in their diet, whereas those in northern Europe do make use of reindeer milk. In other words, about 10,000 years ago there was a genetic change, inherited by Europeans, that enabled them to digest milk as adults.

Genetically, we are very similar to the hunter-gatherers of the late Palaeolithic, but this does not mean that our evolution has not continued during the past 10,000 years. The evidence[24] suggests the opposite. However, the pace of genetic change is outstripped by the circumstances on the ground. There were big changes in human diet as a result of the Neolithic revolution, and there were big changes in the environment (see below). This has led some scholars to suggest that we humans now suffer from **evolutionary discordance** – a mismatch between the situation that our bodies have evolved to respond to and the situation that we face now. Our genetic makeup reflects an evolutionary compromise between multiple, competing selective pressures. Our physiology is therefore a reflection of adaptations that must function simultaneously in concert, and that mutually and intimately affect one another. (This is sometimes called **co-adaptation.**) The discordance hypothesis attempts to assess the disjunction between the ancestral environments and the ones we live in now, and to predict points of vulnerability due to the rapidity of environmental change. In particular, several important chronic degenerative diseases have been interpreted as "diseases of civilization" because they appear to result from this disjunction.[25] A number of dietary complications and diseases are thought to be due to this phenomenon.

Given that humans colonized lands that were very different from that of their remote ancestors, it is not surprising that there have been genetic changes in relation to climate, diet, and disease. The question that most concerns us here is the following: have there been any genetic changes in man's instinctive economic outlook? The answer is probably NO, for the following reason: the microeconomic behaviour of humans is similar to that of other animals, as we shall see in Chapter 2. Therefore, in tracing human economic evolution, we need to think in cultural terms.

Human cultural evolution

It used to be thought that human cultural evolution was primarily an aspect of biological evolution, as is the case with other animals. Differences in the lifestyles of current hunter-gatherers could be explained in terms of genetic or environmental differences, and differences in beliefs, values, and skills through teaching, observation, and learning, but are these sufficient to account for the variation among human societies? Richardson and Boyd[26] argue convincingly that this cannot be the case. Human cultural evolution involves processes that are very different from those of biological evolution, although the results are still ultimately subject to natural selection. For example, modern microeconomic theory is a product of human cultural evolution, but if the economic theory is flawed, the consequences could be severe. In the end, Mother Nature will be the judge.

Tool using and cultural exchange are important aspects of human behaviour, but they are also seen in many other animals. What sets humans apart from other species is language. So far as we know, no other species have this type of representational communication. Information that is made obvious in a physical manner, and is not part of a procedure, requires **explicit knowledge**, or knowledge that something is the case, as distinct from **procedural knowledge** or knowhow. Evidence of **explicit representations** made by early mankind comes from discoveries of maps and cave paintings. The oldest known cave painting is that of the Chauvet Cave, dating to around 30,000 BC. The earliest known maps are of the heavens, not the earth. Dots dating to 16,500 BC found on the walls of the Lascaux caves map out part of the night sky, including the three bright stars of the Summer Triangle asterism and the Pleiades star cluster. The Cuevas de El Castillo in Spain contain a dot map of the Corona Borealis constellation dating from 12,000 BC.[27]

The Neolithic revolution

It is widely thought that the origins of language relate closely to the origins of modern human behaviour, although there is little agreement about the details. Theories abound,[28] although archaeological evidence does provide some clues.[29] However, it is difficult to imagine how people could develop agriculture without using language.

The term Neolithic revolution was coined by Gordon Childe.[30] By this term he did not intend to imply the kind of revolution that we think of in historical terms. He was referring to a revolution in the human way of life, from a nomadic existence to a settled existence that became possible with the domestication of plants and animals. This revolution has occurred among different peoples at different times, and even today there exist people who have not made this transition.

As we have seen, the indigenous peoples of North America, such as the Inuit (Eskimos) hunted caribou, but did not herd tame them for milking. Even faced with the same animal in a similar environment as the North Eurasian peoples, they did not bring these animals into semi-domestication. This difference is probably due to genetic differences between these two peoples of differing origin. Thus whereas the Inuit diet is composed of marine mammals, fish, caribou, small game, birds, and plants, the Sami depend on herded reindeer for milk and meat, and on fishing, gathering plants, and hunting small game and birds. Thus, in these northern extreme conditions we see (until recently) humans on the verge of the Neolithic revolution.

In warmer parts of the world, domestication of animals and plants began much earlier. Dogs were domesticated about 17,000 years ago, and would have been useful as guard dogs, and as an aid to hunters. Sheep and goats were domesticated about 12,500 years ago.[31] It is worth noting that these animals – dogs, sheep, and goats – could have been kept by nomadic peoples, herded along when the group was on the move. Pigs were domesticated somewhat later, about 11,000 years ago, but these would be kept by people in settled villages. Similarly, cattle were first domesticated about 10,000 years ago.

Domestication of plants began at different times in different places. For example, wild yams (*Dioscorea*) were gathered by hunter-gatherers, but it was usually necessary to remove their toxic alkaloids by boiling. Domestication of yams developed independently in tropical America, South-east Asia, and West Africa.[32] Archaeological evidence shows that capsicum peppers were eaten 9,000 years ago in the Americas but these were probably wild plants. Domestication of peppers is thought to have started 7,000 years ago, in two separate locations. *Phaseolus* beans are native to the Americas, and archaeological evidence indicates that they were cultivated some 8,000–9,000 years ago. A similar story can be told about groundnuts. However, the Neolithic revolution is usually exemplified by the domestication of wheat and barley in Egypt.

About 11,000 years ago there were established villages in the Eastern Mediterranean that relied on a combination of hunting and intensive gathering. Wild grasses in that area had edible seeds, and a man with a flint-bladed sickle could gather two pounds of grain in one hour.[33] The inhabitants probably discovered that by leaving some plants to disperse their seeds, they were more likely to have plants to harvest the next year. It is a small step to plant some seeds yourself. Cultivation of crops from this area (often called the Fertile Crescent) spread rapidly throughout the Mediterranean, reaching central Europe in 2,000 years, and Britain and Scandinavia in another 2,000 years. Early Neolithic people went to a great deal of trouble to prepare wheat and barley. The edible part of the grain (consisting of the embryo and the endosperm) had to be separated from its protective coating (the bran and the chaff). Archaeological investigations, in Egypt, Syria, Iraq, and the Jordan valley, show that this was done by heating the grain on hot stones. Cooking became easier with the invention of pottery. But pottery is not of much use to nomadic people. It is too heavy to carry around, and it breaks easily. The first pottery cooking vessels were made in Japan 14,000 years ago. By this time some Japanese people had settled in fishing villages on the coast, where they exploited the marine resources.[34] Pottery was used for cooking purposes in the near East 8,000 years ago, and in the Americas by 3,500 years ago.[35]

A big advantage of grain is that it can be stored, but a disadvantage is that such stores cannot be easily moved. Therefore, communities that cultivated grain had to secure **territory** on which they could live and grow and store their crops. The inhabitants of such settlements would find it more difficult to go hunting, because they would soon exhaust the game supply in their area. Unlike nomadic people, they could not follow migrating animals, or move to new hunting areas. To have a good supply of meat, they would have to keep animals in semi-captivity, and they would have to tame them. In other words, they would have to invest in animal domestication. For these, and other, reasons, their diet was bound to change.

The changes in human diet during the Neolithic period would vary from region to region. Those growing crops inland would eat much more carbohydrate than their Palaeolithic ancestors, those keeping reindeer, goats, or cows would eat more dairy produce, while those living on the coast would have a relatively smaller change in their diet. Human food is a result of human behaviour, and there is no doubt that there was a large evolutionary change in human food as a result of the Neolithic revolution. This change had three possible and important effects:

- it changed humans genetically;
- it changed the environment;
- it changed the human lifestyle, with consequences for health and reproduction.

Turning now to the changing environment during the past 10,000 years, a major impact of agriculture has been deforestation. Early Neolithic farmers would clear land for cultivation, using a slash and burn approach, and this practice carries on to this day. Wood was the main source of fuel for thousands of years, and as the human population grew, their appetite for wood grew. Trees were felled to provide wood for fires, buildings, and ships. The vast woodlands and forests that appeared at the end of the last ice age are now severely attenuated. Not only has this changed the landscape in many places, but it is also thought to have had an effect upon the climate.[36]

Agriculture also had other effects upon the environment. In Mesopotamia over the past 6,000 years, the development of irrigation systems has led to a considerable increase in the agricultural area, but since the fourth millennium, large area losses due to irrigation mistakes (salinization) have occurred. Deforestation and erosion processes are known to have originated in several regions of the Mediterranean area over the past 7,000 years.

How did these environmental changes affect mankind? The **life expectancy** of Palaeolithic hunter-gatherers was not much different from that of 18th century Europeans. Life expectancy is the average number of years a human has before death, conventionally calculated from the time of birth (note that this measure includes infant deaths). For Neanderthal man, the life expectancy was 20 years, and for Palaeolithic hunter-gatherers, it was 33 years. So *Homo sapiens* was doing better than *Homo neanderthalensis*, and the latter became extinct. During the Neolithic period, however, human life expectancy dropped significantly (to 20 years). In classical Greece and Rome, it was 20–30 years, but in pre-Columbian North America it was 25–35 years. In medieval Britain, life expectancy was 20–30 years, and in the early 20th century it was 30–40 years. Now, the current world average is 67 years, and rising.[37] So we can see that the Neolithic revolution was accompanied by a marked drop in life expectancy. Of course, the change to an agricultural way of life occurred in different places at different times, so the question is – did the same effect occur at these different times? The answer is yes. Wherever and whenever people changed from a hunter-gatherer to an agricultural way of life, life expectancy declined.[38] The evidence suggests that farmers suffered higher rates of infection due to the increase in the size and permanence of human settlements, poorer nutrition due to reduced meat intake, and greater interference with mineral absorption by the cereal-based diet. Consequently, Neolithic farmers were shorter and had a lower life expectancy relative to their hunter-gatherer ancestors. However, there was a rise in the birth rate[39] and a large population increase.

In summary, the Neolithic revolution started in different places at different times – and in some places it never started, the inhabitants remaining hunter-gatherers to this day. The revolution brought about a large increase in the human population and reproductive success, but the lifespan of most individuals was reduced. This reduction was partly due to excessive consumption of foods to which the people were not evolutionarily adjusted, and partly to changes in lifestyle, such as living in one place. Nomadic peoples move on, and to some extent leave their enemies behind. The longer you stay in one place the more you attract rats and mice, and other disease-bearing creatures. The more you stay in one place, the more the population increases, and the greater the chance of cross-infection. The advantages of staying in one place are that pottery can be made and used for more efficient cooking. Food can be stored against lean times, and various community activities can develop. Finally, settled territorial existence led to profound social changes, and these changes led to a marked change in the human economic situation.

Forms of exchange

Primitive agriculture leads to domestication of plants and animals, and to more complex economic organization. Except when working individuals consume the fruits of their own labours, the products of human labour are distributed by means of exchange – the practice of giving and receiving valuable objects and services. Most hunter-gatherers practised some form of reciprocal exchange, the giving of goods and services that is not contingent on any definite receipt of goods and services in return. This practice persists to this day, in our societies, at Christmas and other festivities. The giving is based on a general understanding that there will be some eventual reciprocity.

Reciprocal exchange is open to invasion by cheats, or free-loaders. They receive favours from others, but do not reciprocate. In some cases, such as the giving of food or clothing to children, no reciprocation is expected, but a roughly symmetrical reciprocity is expected amongst adults. In societies practising reciprocal exchange free-loaders are subject to subtle forms of disapproval, but demands are not made upon them in particular cases. It is usually part of the ethos of reciprocal exchange to deny that any balance is being calculated. According to anthropologist Marvin Harris,

> Boastfulness and acknowledgement of generosity is incompatible with the basic etiquette of reciprocal exchange. Among the Semai of Central Malaya, no one even says "thank you" for the meat received … Having struggled all day to lug the carcass of a pig home through the jungle heat, the hunter allows his prize to be cut up into exactly equal portions, which are then given away to the entire group … to express gratitude for the portion received

indicated that you are the kind of person who calculates how much you are giving and taking... To call attention to one's generosity is to indicate that others are in debt to you and that you expect them to repay you. It is repugnant to egalitarian peoples even to suggest that they have been treated generously.[40]

Reciprocal exchange is more likely to occur amongst people who are genetically related, partly because hunter-gatherer groups are usually inter-related, and partly because it is human nature to favour your kin. There is some evidence indicating that the extent of reciprocal exchange is in fact related to kinship distance in hunter-gatherer societies. Once people become settled, and community size increases, then simple reciprocity breaks down. Reciprocal exchange works well when productivity is not over-encouraged, and the supply of food remains stable. If the human population increases, more food is required, and individual providers tend to be praised and encouraged. Successful providers acquire a reputation, and their status in the community changes.

It is noteworthy that many hunter-gatherer communities under-exploit their food resources. For example,

> Although Hazda, in common with probably all other human societies, do not eat all the types of animal available to them – they reject civet, monitor lizard, snake, terrapin, among others – they do eat an unusually wide range of animals.... In spite of the large number of species which they are both able to hunt and regard as edible, the Hazda do not kill very many animals and it is probable that even in the radically reduced area they occupied in 1960 more animals could have been killed of every species without endangering the survival of any species in question.[41]

It is a short step from simple egalitarian reciprocal exchange to egalitarian redistribution. Imagine a community where some members go hunting, others gather wild plants, and others cultivate the land. Then they all get together and pool their resources. Instead of a producer sharing what has been gained that day, the producers now give their gains to a central pool, and somebody then distributes the food throughout the community. That somebody has a special status and responsibility in deciding who gets what. Politics has now entered the arena. Of course, pooling probably always existed within the family, because children do not help themselves, but are assisted or supervised by an adult. But in a wider arena pooling involves a shift in the social order. This shift has been a major topic of discussion amongst anthropologists, and it is clear that the repercussions have been different in different communities. However, there is one effect that is of importance to us, and that is the increase in productivity that is heralded by this type of change in social organization. Once a person takes responsibility for distributing food, that person is not only marked out as different, that person has an incentive to encourage productivity. When things are bad, the focus is on the distributor. When things are good, that person acquires a halo. So there gradually develops a political vested interest in increasing productivity.

To quote Marshal Sahlins

> Agriculture not only raised society above the distribution of natural food resources, it allowed Neolithic communities to maintain a high degree of social order where the requirements of human existence were absent from the natural order. Enough food could be harvested in some seasons to sustain the people while no food would grow at all; the consequent stability of social life was critical for its material enlargement. Culture went on then from triumph to triumph, in a kind of progressive contravention of the biological law of the minimum, until it proved it could support human life in outer space – where even gravity and oxygen were naturally lacking.[42]

In other words, while nomadic Palaeolithic hunter-gatherers could move on when things got bad, their settled Neolithic descendants had to devise ways of storing food, and distributing stored food. If the special person who has the responsibility of distributing pooled food is not themselves a food producer, then we have the beginnings of what Jared Diamond calls a kleptocracy.[43]

> chiefdoms introduced the dilemma fundamental to all centrally governed, non egalitarian societies. At best, they do good by providing expensive services impossible to contract for on an individual basis. At worst, they function unabashedly as

kleptocrats, transferring net wealth from commoners to upper classes. These noble and selfish functions are inextricably linked.

Once the supply of food is under political control, things start to change. Firstly, accounts are kept. In a system where productivity is encouraged, there has to be some kind of account of who produced what. Agricultural people can often benefit from increasing production, provided they do not endanger their food supplies. They can afford to admire and encourage those who are big providers, provided things do not get out of control. To control productivity some kind of policing is required. Whoever produces must contribute, but someone must also safeguard the means of production. This kind of situation leads to stratified redistribution, with the controllers at the top, the producers in the middle, and the consumers at the bottom.

Exchange amongst unrelated (non-kin) groups usually takes place at some kind of marketplace. In the absence of money, goods and services are bartered. There is bargaining between the opposing parties, each trying to maximize their profitability. If the barter exchanges are not direct, then some sort of accounts must be kept. There must be mutual trust, or some kind of policing. This type of barter market can work satisfactorily if relatively few commodities are involved in the exchange. A society that has some form of all-purpose money can operate a price market. The producers sell their goods in exchange for money, and use money to purchase other goods or services. The main advantage of a price market is that it can handle many commodities in a mixed economy. Another advantage is that it facilitates trade with strangers, with whom no elaborate trust arrangements exist. Traditionally, money has been regarded as a portable, recognizable material. It has a certain legality that makes it divisible and convertible, and confers wide generality of use. In recent times, however, we have started to move away from money as a physical object of exchange. Bank accounts and credit cards enable us to promise each other that we will pay our debts at some time in the future. In this respect we seem to be returning to some features of reciprocal exchange.

Points to remember

- Humans are animals, and human behaviour, including economic behaviour, has been the product of evolutionary pressures that are the result of natural selection, whether they be cultural or genetic.

- The characteristic life-history strategy of humans is to care not only for their personal lifestyle, but also for that of their offspring, and relatives.
- For natural selection to favour reciprocal altruism, the individuals must have sufficient opportunities for reciprocation, they must be able to recognize each other individually and remember their obligations, and they must be motivated to reciprocate. These conditions are found in primitive human societies, and reciprocal altruism has played an important role in human evolution.
- Cultural exchange of various sorts occurs in many animal species, but it has become prevalent amongst humans as a result of the evolution of language.
- Genetically, humans have changed little over the past 60,000 years but the changes in human diet as a result of the Neolithic revolution, have led to some evolutionary discordance – a mismatch between the situation that our bodies have evolved to respond to and the situation that we face now.
- Early humans practised some form of *reciprocal exchange*, the giving of goods and services that is not contingent on any definite receipt of goods and services in return.

Further reading

Cohen, M.N. (1989) *Health and the Rise of Civilization.* Yale University Press, New Haven.

Diamond, Jared (1998) *Guns, Germs and Steel.* Vintage, London.

Harris, M. (1985) *Culture, People, Nature,* 4th edn. Harper and Row, New York.

Richardson, P.J. and Boyd, R. (2005) *Not by Genes Alone. How Culture Transformed Human Evolution.* University of Chicago Press, Chicago, IL.

Robson, A.J. and Kaplan, H. (2003) The evolution of human life expectancy and intelligence in hunter-gatherer economies. *Am. Econ. Rev.,* 93(1), 150–169.

Sahlins, M. (1974) *Stone Age Economics.* Tavistock Publications, London.

Trivers, R. (1971) The evolution of reciprocal altruism. *Quart. Rev. Biol.,* 46, 35–57.

Essential reading

Gaudy, John (1999) Hunter-gatherers and the mythology of the market. In Lee, R. and Daly, R. (eds) *The Cambridge Encyclopedia of Hunters and Gatherers.* Cambridge University Press, Cambridge.

2
The Economic Behaviour of the Individual

In Chapter 1 we focused on the evolution of *Homo sapiens*. In this chapter we focus on the individual, that is *Homo economicus*, an imaginary, "rational", individual with a long history.

The term "economic man" was first used by John Stuart Mill in the late 19th century. *Homo economicus* is seen as "rational" in the sense that a relevant **utility function** is maximized given perceived opportunities. That is, the individual seeks to attain very specific and predetermined gains with the least possible cost. In other words, *Homo economicus* bases choices on a consideration of a very personal utility function. This view has been criticized by anthropologists,[1] sociologists, and various economists, but it is not our aim to recapitulate these well-worn arguments. In this chapter we would like to paint a much wider *biological* picture.

A biological approach

The biologist John Goss-Custard[2] studied foraging in the redshank (*Tringa totanus*), a wading bird that hunts for food along the seashore and on mudflats. He found that when these birds are feeding exclusively on polychaete worms (*Nereis diversicolor* and *Nephthys hombergi*), they tend to pass over the smaller worms and to select those over a certain size. Their size preference is influenced by the rate at which they encounter the larger worms but not by their encounter rate with small worms. This finding is consistent with the view that the redshank's foraging strategy is designed to maximize energy profitability; that is, they select those worms that provide the

greatest amount of energy per unit of energy expended on foraging. The smaller worms are not so profitable because of the relatively
low net energy returns on time spent foraging for them. Taken at
face value, these results might suggest that redshanks make decisions
about which prey to take on the basis of energy **trade-offs**, and this
view is consistent with the body of **optimal foraging theory**.[3] However, Goss-Custard also found that when the amphipod crustacean
Corophium was available in addition to polychaete worms, the birds
tended to select *Corophium* some of the time. He was able to dis-
count the possibility that the habitat typical of *Corophium* was one
in which polychaete worms were harder to find because he observed
that some birds concentrated on worms while the majority was feeding on *Corophium*. On the basis of his previous work, Goss-Custard
had formed the hypothesis that redshanks achieved a higher rate of
net energy intake by feeding on *Corophium* than by taking worms.
However, when he came to examine the energy content of the prey[4]
and the energy costs of obtaining prey he found that the birds
would have obtained between two and three times more energy per
minute by taking worms exclusively than they obtained by feeding
on *Corophium*. Clearly, energy was not the only factor relevant to
foraging redshanks when *Corophium* was available. Presumably, the
Corophium contain something other than energy that is important to
the redshank. Clearly, the redshank has choices to make, and as we
shall see, its choices are made on a "rational" basis.

According to standard microeconomic theory, there are two basic
principles of human economic decision-making.[5] The first is that
it must be rational, and the second is that it must involve some
evaluation of the pros and cons of the situation. The basis of **rational decision-making** is that it should be self-consistent, a property
that usually involves *transitivity of choice*.[6] Suppose a person has to
choose between options A, B, and C. If A is preferred to B, and B to C,
then it is rational to expect that A will be preferred to C. We can now
write a consistent order of preference, $A > B > C$. These relationships
among A, B, and C are said to be transitive. If $A > B$ and $B > C$, but A is
not preferred to C, then the decision to choose C above A is irrational,
and the relationships among A, B, and C are intransitive. Economists
base their theory upon the concept of the rational economic person, and this implies that all preference relationships are transitive.[7]
Transitivity of choice has also been demonstrated in other animals,[8]

but this phenomenon is not the only aspect of rationality that is important to economists. They tend to assume that rationality has to do with reasoning, and this might imply that animals that demonstrate transitivity are capable of reasoning.[9] However, recent research suggests that different species of animal may achieve transitivity of choice in different ways.

The name given to the quantity that is maximized in the choice behaviour of the rational economic person is **utility**. I may obtain a certain amount of utility from buying china for my collection, a certain amount from sport and a certain amount from reading books. In spending my time and money on these things, I choose in a way that maximizes the amount of satisfaction or utility that I obtain in return. I am not aware of maximizing utility, but (if I am rational) I appear to behave in a way that maximizes utility. Thus, utility is a notional measure of the psychological value of goods, leisure, and so on. It is called a notional measure because we do not know whether or not it is explicitly represented in people's choice behaviour. We only assume that they behave as if utility is maximized.[10]

The animal as an economic consumer

We saw above that redshanks foraging on mudflats sometimes prefer *Corophium* to polychaete worms, even though they obtain much less energy from *Corophium*. We conclude that the *Corophium* must provide something other than energy that is of importance to the redshank. What might an economist have to say about this situation? To simplify matters, we will refer to the redshank prey as worms and shrimps, and we will assume that each prey provides a certain amount of energy and a certain amount of some unknown nutrient. The energy and nutrient content are present in different proportions in the two prey, as shown in Figure 2.1. This means that the consequences of eating the two prey are different and can be portrayed as different arrows in a diagram representing the possible consequences of choice behaviour.

The economist would next ask about the relative price of worms and shrimps. Redshanks have to expend more energy to obtain shrimps than to obtain the equivalent energy return from worms. The price of shrimps in energy terms is about twice that of worms. Figure 2.1 shows how many worms and shrimps a bird could obtain

	Worms	Shrimps
Energy	7	3
Nutrient	7	3

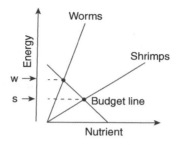

Figure 2.1   Consequences of eating worms and shrimps in terms of energy and nutrient gained

Note: The budget line is based upon the energy prices of worms and shrimps.

for a given amount of energy spent on foraging. This is equivalent to the amount of goods A and B that a shopper could obtain for a given amount of money. The amount of energy an animal has at the time of foraging acts as a constraint on what it can purchase. The energy obtained by foraging is not immediately available for use because the food has to be digested, just as the money a person earns by working is not immediately available to spend. The budget line in Figure 2.1 represents the constraints on foraging that are imposed by the bird's available energy. This means that, within a given period of time, the bird cannot obtain more worms and shrimps than the quantities represented inside the triangle formed by the budget line.

The next question is what utility does a redshank derive from energy and the nutrient? The utility of such commodities usually obeys a law of diminishing returns; that is, if an animal already has a good supply of energy, a little extra does not add much to the utility. If the animal is short of energy, however, then that same small amount of energy will make a large contribution to utility. The same considerations commonly apply to human economics. Thus, I may derive a certain amount of satisfaction or utility from my large china collection. If I add one more piece of china to my collection, then

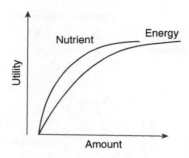

Figure 2.2 Hypothetical utility functions for nutrient and energy

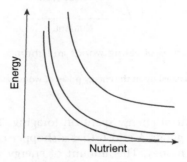

Figure 2.3 Iso-utility functions for nutrient and energy
Source: Based upon Figure 2.2.

I will increase my satisfaction by a small amount. If I had a smaller collection, however, then adding that same piece would increase my satisfaction by a larger amount.

If we take hypothetical utility functions for the nutrient and energy (Figure 2.2), we can combine the iso-utility curves that join all points of equal utility (Figure 2.3). Thus the redshank may obtain the same utility from a large amount of energy combined with a small amount of the nutrient as from a small amount of energy combined with a large amount of the nutrient. The shape of the iso-utility curve is determined by the shape of the corresponding utility functions. In terms of the human economic analogy, I might derive the same total utility from purchasing two pieces of china and one tennis ball as from one piece of china and six tennis balls. For this reason, economists often call iso-utility curves **indifference curves**.

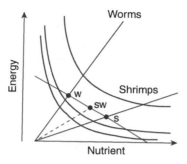

Figure 2.4   Iso-utility functions from Figure 2.3 superimposed on Figure 2.1
Note: The dotted line indicates the best possible mixture of worms and shrimps, assuming that there is no cost of changing between them.

Suppose we now combine the budget line (Figure 2.1) and the iso-utility curves. We can now see that certain combinations of worms and shrimps will yield higher utility than others (Figure 2.4). The least utility is obtained by foraging for worms alone (w), more is obtained from shrimps alone (s), but even more is obtained by a certain combination of worms and shrimps (sw). Two main factors affect the combination that yields the highest utility: the shape of the iso-utility curves (determined by the utility functions) and the slope of the budget line (determined by the relative process of the two commodities).

In human consumer economics, if a person has more money to spend, then more goods can be purchased and there is a parallel shift in the budget line, as illustrated in Figure 2.3. If the price of a particular item is lowered, then more can be purchased for the same amount of money, and this also has the effect of making the budget triangle larger (see Figure 2.5). However, a price change for a single item alters the slope of the budget line, which does not occur if the overall budget is increased (Figure 2.6). Comparison of Figures 2.5 and 2.6 shows that there is little change in the optimal preference when the overall budget is altered but that changes in price cause a considerable shift in optimal preferences.

In likening an animal to a human economic consumer, we can regard utility as the common currency of decision-making. We distinguish between these concepts and the energy cost or price associated with particular activities or goods. Although energy cost is a common factor in the alternative possible activities in the examples

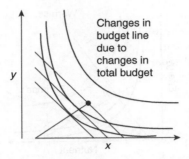

Figure 2.5   Different budget lines result from differences in the amount of energy initially available to the animal
Note: The optimal preference does not change.

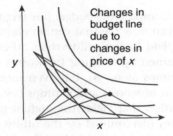

Figure 2.6   Changes in the budget line due to changes in the price of x
Note: There is change in optimal preference.

we have discussed so far, this is not always the case. It is a mistake, therefore, to regard energy as a common currency for decision-making even though it may be a common factor in particular cases. Energy will be a factor common to all alternatives only if energy availability acts as a constraint in the circumstances being considered. A human economic example may help to make this distinction clear.

The supermarket analogy

Suppose a person enters a supermarket to purchase a variety of goods. As we have seen, utility functions will be associated with each possible item of purchase, and the utility of particular goods will depend upon the shopper's preferences and experience. Factors such as the palatability, visual attractiveness, list of ingredients, and so on will influence the utility associated with food items. The concept of utility enables very different items to be compared.

A person may obtain the same utility from a packet of mixed herbs as from a bottle of soda. Utility is thus the currency by which different items are evaluated. However, another currency common to all items is money. This will be important if the shopper has a limited amount to spend because it acts as a constraint upon the amount he or she can purchase. However, although every item in the supermarket has a marked price, money is not always the relevant constraint. A shopper who is in a great hurry may carry more money than can be spent in the time available. Time is now the constraint that bites, and it may be that the shopper can choose among bottles of soda more quickly than among different packets of mixed herbs. Time taken to choose each item will determine the slope of the time–budget line, and it may turn out that the shopper's choice when pressed for time is different from that of the shopper with limited cash.

The lesson to be learned from this example is that many possible constraints act upon an animal's choice behaviour. These constraints may vary with circumstances, but it is only the constraint that bites at the time that is important. For this reason, time and energy should not be confused with utility or with cost (in terms of **fitness**). In drawing the analogy between an animal and a human economic consumer, cost is equivalent to utility, energy is equivalent to money, and time is equivalent to time. The animal can earn energy (money) by foraging (working) and may spend it upon various other activities. Over and above the basic continuous level of metabolic (subsistence) expenditure, the animal can save energy (bank money) by **hoarding** food or depositing fat, or it can spend it upon various activities including foraging (working). When the price of activities is high, the animal is subject to a tight energy-budget constraint, and when the price is reduced the animal experiences an increase in real income and the budget constraint is relaxed.

If we have a limited amount of money to spend on a variety of goods and activities, we often partition it among the different purposes. We usually review our expenditure over a particular period of time such as a day, a week, or a year, and we call this a budget. The budgeting process may occur in advance of any expenditure, or it may occur in retrospect. In the one case we allocate particular sums to particular purposes, while in the other we review the expenditure that has already occurred. In either case, the notion of budgeting implies a certain discipline in spending money.

As we have seen, money in human consumer economics can be seen as analogous to energy in animal behaviour. It is natural, therefore, to ask whether or not animals have energy budgets. However, we have seen also that energy is only one type of constraint that impinges on animal behaviour. Another important constraint is time, and we can also ask whether time budgets are relevant to animal behaviour. A time or energy budget should not simply be an account of how an animal spent its time or energy. An animal whose use of time and energy was completely chaotic would have no budget. However, we can expect that natural selection will design animals in a way that their available time and energy is put to maximum use. It seems reasonable, therefore, to expect that animals will treat time and energy as valuable resources and will budget accordingly.

Biologist Bernd Heinrich[11] likened the foraging bumblebee (*Bombus*) to a shopper:

> A bee starting to forage in a meadow with many different flowers faces a task not unlike that confronting an illiterate shopper pushing a cart down the aisle of a supermarket. Directly or indirectly, both try to get the most value for their money. Neither knows beforehand the precise contents of the packages on the shelf or in the meadow. But they learn by experience.

The bees are dependent upon flowers for the energy required to rear the young, but they may have to expend considerable amounts of energy in foraging. Bumblebees are able to exist in cold climates by virtue of their remarkable themoregulatory physiology. They can maintain a high body temperature at a low environmental temperature. This enables them to be active, although it involves a high rate of energy expenditure. They can conserve energy by greatly reducing their activity level and conserving heat. When food resources from flowers are scarce, the bees nevertheless manage to make a profit by foraging slowly. When food is abundant, they raise their body temperature and forage rapidly. Thus, they budget their energy expenditure in accordance with the prevailing circumstances.

A foraging bumblebee spends most of its time travelling. In moving from flower to flower, bees try to keep their flight time and distance to a minimum. They fly between 11 and 20 km h^{-1} and spend only 2–4 minutes inside the nest between foraging trips. Simple calculations[12] show that the time budget is more important than the energy budget for a foraging bumblebee. Suppose, for example, that one bee has flowers close to the nest and can forage there continuously, while another bee is foraging 3 km from the nest. If the second bee flies at 15 km h^{-1}, it must spend 24 minutes travelling time per trip. Foraging on fireweed, both bees could collect a honey crop-full (about 30 milligrams of sugar) of nectar in about 10 minutes. The commuting bee would thus collect 30 milligrams of sugar in 34 minutes but would expend about 3 milligrams in flight metabolism. Thus, commuting takes up about two-thirds of the time per trip but only one-tenth of the energy. The bee foraging close to the nest would obtain 102 milligrams of sugar in a foraging trip of the same duration. Thus, to make commuting worthwhile, the flowers far away from the nest would have to be 3.4 times more rewarding than those close by. Bumblebees change their foraging behaviour in response to changes in nectar abundance. The more nectar they find per flower, the more they search other flowers in the vicinity. Heinrich carried out experiments in which he laid screens of bridal veil over some patches of clover and left others unscreened. The bees depleted the nectar in the unscreened clover, but that in the screened clover accumulated. When the screening was removed, the bees could visit both rich and poor areas of clover. In nectar-rich areas they probed about 12 florets per head and made short flights between heads. In areas of low nectar the bees probed only about two florets on each flower head and made longer flights between heads. In this way the bumblebees concentrated their foraging in the more profitable areas.

   The energy costs of foraging depend partly upon the environmental temperature. When foraging on fireweed the bees stop for only one or two seconds at each flower and remove tiny drops of nectar with a dab of the tongue. On the other types of flower, however, they may remain a number of minutes. While perching on a flower, the bees do not allow their flight mechanism to cool, but they keep it at flight temperature so that they are ready to fly without delay. During prolonged perching they maintain the thorax at a temperature of about 32°C by shivering, but they do not waste energy heating the abdomen, which is not involved in powered flight. At environmental temperatures of about 25°C, it is not necessary to heat the thorax during periods of inactivity, but below this temperature the bee has to pay progressively more to maintain efficient foraging. Some flower species produce more nectar than others, and it is possible to calculate the relative costs of foraging on different types of flower at different temperatures. Bumblebees forage on the profitable rhododendron flowers over a wide range of temperature, but they do not forage on lambkill and wild cherry at low temperatures because they cannot forage quickly enough to offset the extra energy required for thermoregulation.[13]

Bumblebee foraging illustrates how time and energy act as constraints upon foraging efficiency. When the bees have to travel some distance to find productive flowers, then time becomes a limiting factor, and it is worthwhile for the bee to expend energy in order to save time. When foraging on relatively unproductive flowers or when foraging at a low temperature, the bee may take more time in order to save energy.

Time and energy budgets in animals

Interactions between time and energy are important in many aspects of animal behaviour. The animal has to budget for each particular type of activity and for the particular consequences of each. In such circumstances trade-off is inevitable, and has been demonstrated many times in animal behaviour. In addition, the animal must budget for the **cost of changing** from one activity to another. When an animal changes from one activity to another, there may be a cost involved in the process of changing. For example, a pigeon feeding in a cornfield will become thirsty as a result of eating dry seeds. It may have to fly a mile to obtain water. In addition to the physiological cost of the journey, the bird will spend some time simply travelling from the feeding place to the drinking place. During this period it will not receive any of the benefits of feeding or drinking. Moreover, there may be risks involved in the journey, such as exposure to hawks or farmers with guns. Thus, the cost of changing is the decrement of fitness that arises during the period in which the animal is changing from one activity to another and receiving benefits from neither. The cost may involve loss of valuable time, expenditure of energy, or risk from predators. It can be shown theoretically that the cost of changing should be budgeted as if it were part of the cost of the activity that is about to be performed.[14]

We can distinguish between the *instantaneous cost* that arises within each unit of the relevant period of time and the *cumulative cost* that occurs over the whole of the period under consideration. The important thing is that a change in behaviour is worthwhile if the cumulative cost a short time after changing is less than it would have been if the animal had not changed behaviour at all. It has been shown by experiment[15] that, when the cost of changing is high, doves change between feeding and drinking less often than they would otherwise do. Experiments show that these birds do indeed allocate the cost of changing to the cost of the behaviour that is about to be performed.[16] They do not change their behaviour until they have accounted for this cost. The patterns of feeding and drinking in doves altered in a predictable manner when the cost of changing from one to the other was increased in terms of time or of energy expenditure required.

In addition to minute-to-minute considerations, animals take a more global account of their time and energy budgets. In general, we can expect that behaviour that has the prime function of promoting the survival of the individual will take precedence over behaviour that promotes other aspects of fitness, such as territorial mating and parental behaviour. However, species vary considerably. Some aspects of behaviour are essential, but others such as thermoregulatory behaviour may be important only when physiological mechanisms cannot cope. Thus, drinking is a daily necessity for some species, but other species can manage without drinking at all.

Each activity has value in terms of fitness, and animals must be designed to allocate priorities to activities in a general way, as well as from minute to minute. This problem can be approached by considering a measure of the cost to an animal of abstaining from each activity in its natural repertoire.[17] If an animal did no feeding, for instance, the cost would be high, but if it abstained from grooming the cost might be relatively low. An animal that had a high motivational tendency for both feeding and grooming but did not have time to do both would sacrifice less, in terms of fitness, if it devoted its available time to feeding.

Suppose an animal fills its typical day with useful activities. In an environment that was much the same from day to day, the animal would adjust its activities to the time available. Suppose, however, there is a change in the environment such that it now takes very much longer to obtain the normal amount of food. The animal can respond to the changed circumstances by spending the same amount of time feeding as before and settling for less food. Alternatively, it could insist on the same amount of food as usual, or it could compromise between the two extremes. If the animal spent a long time obtaining the usual amount of food, then there would be less time available for all the other activities in its repertoire. These would have to be squashed into the remaining time. The extent to which an activity resists squashing can be represented by a single parameter, called *resilience*.[18] In the case where the animal feeds for the normal amount of time and ends up with a reduced food intake the **resilience** of feeding is relatively low because feeding has not compressed the other activities even though the animal's hunger is increased. In the case where the animal insists on the normal amount of food, the resilience of feeding is relatively high because feeding ousts the other activities from the time available without itself being curtailed in any way.

Behavioural **resilience** is a measure of the extent to which each activity can be squashed in terms of time by other activities in the animal's repertoire. It also reflects the importance of an activity in a long-term sense. During periods when time is a budget constraint, activities with low resilience will tend to be ignored. Indeed, if an activity completely disappears from an animal's repertoire when time is rationed, we might call it a luxury or leisure activity. Behavioural resilience has been measured directly in few cases because of the practical difficulties involved. It is necessary to keep a record of the behaviour around the clock for a number of days in a situation where available time can be manipulated. Observations of this kind have been carried out on female canaries (*Serinus canarias*).[19] The aim of the study was to investigate how photoperiod length affects the activity and hormonal balance of the birds. By manipulating photoperiods, the experimenter effectively was altering the time available for activity because canaries are inactive in the dark. It was found that the birds spend the same amount of time feeding on short days as on long days but that they fed more efficiently on long days. During long days the birds expend more energy in various activities, so this result is not entirely unexpected. Birds kept on long days spent more daytime inactive and sleeping than birds on short days. Since the birds can sleep at night, it seems most likely that birds kept on long days filled spare time with sleep. This view is supported by the fact that birds that were building a nest spent less time sleeping during the day.[20]

It is possible to calculate the time available for nest building after time necessary for feeding, grooming, and travelling from place to place had been taken into account. It turns out that there is adequate time for nest building on long days but barely enough time on short days. The interpretation of the observations is complicated, however, by the fact that long days stimulate hormone production so that these birds are more motivated to build a nest than birds kept on short days. The nest-building behaviour of birds kept on long days is more efficient than that of birds on short days, and less time is wasted on unnecessarily repetitious gathering and building movements. Thus, although resilience is a concept that is theoretically distinct from that of **motivation**,[21] it is difficult to isolate its effects in studies of time budgets.

However, resilience can be measured indirectly by means of **demand functions**.[22] These are used by economists to express the relationship between the price and the consumption of a commodity. For example, when the price of coffee is increased in the supermarket, people continue to buy about the same amount as before, perhaps a little less. As the price of fruit is increased, however, the demand for fruit falls off. When the price of fresh fish is increased, demand declines markedly. Presumably, people are willing to pay more to maintain their normal coffee-drinking habits. Demand for coffee is said to be *inelastic*. If the price of fresh fish increases, however, people tend to buy less and to switch to substitute foods such as meat or canned fish. Demand for fish is said to be *elastic*.

Exactly analogous phenomena occur in animal behaviour. If an animal expends a certain amount of energy in a particular activity, then it usually does less of that activity if the energy requirement is increased. Numerous studies have shown that demand functions in animals follow the same general pattern as those of humans.[23] For example, demand for food is inelastic in rats required to work (press a lever) to obtain food rewards. As the work required (lever presses per reward) increased, the rats continue to work for about the same amount of food. However, the elasticity of demand for food pellets increases when sucrose was available as a substitute.

There appears to be a parallel between the demand phenomena of humans and other animals. Elasticity of demand gives an indication of the relative importance of the commodities (or activities) on which the person (or animal) spends his or her money (or energy). There is a close relationship between elasticity of demand and resilience. Thus, demand functions can be used as indirect measures of resilience. If activity A has higher resilience than activity B, then A will tend to show a relatively inelastic demand function and B will show an elastic one. Whereas demand is usually thought of as relating to price (in terms of energy or money), resilience is related to time.

Nearly all animals on this planet exhibit some kind of diurnal rhythm, based upon their internal (molecular) clock(s). There is a fixed amount of time in a day, and most animals spend that time in obtaining food + other activities + sleeping. How this time is allocated among the various possible activities invariably changes with the seasons.[24] All animals have to allocate scarce resources among competing ends. The scarce resources may be energy, nutrients, or time. The competing ends may be growth and reproduction, in the long term; or alternative activities, in the case of short-term decision-making. So the basic economic problems are the same for all animals, including humans.

Animal and human economics

The similarity between human micro-economic behaviour and that of other animals raises various questions. Is human consumer behaviour culturally or genetically based? It could be argued that scarce resources in terms of time, or energy, are the same for most animals, and it is not surprising that it is in their nature to follow what is basically the logic of choice. On the other hand humans are more intelligent, and more sophisticated, as a result of having evolved language. So we might expect there to be considerable cultural influences on the economic behaviour of the individual. One way to tackle this problem is to look at hunter-gatherers. Do hunter-gatherers who have no money, and few possessions, exhibit "classical" economic behaviour?

Now consider the !Kung San, hunter-gatherers that were extensively studied by anthropologist Richard Lee,[25] before their way of life changed for ever. These people lived in the Dobe area of the Kalahari desert in Botswana. Lee found that individuals worked to obtain food that was shared among all members of the group, plus any visitors.

The consumption of each person was the same in relation to their requirements. In other words the food was shared out fairly. The San did not live a hand-to-mouth existence. They might have eaten a little of what they obtained in the field, but most was transported to the camp and shared out. Most of this food could not be eaten right away, but had to be processed. The hunting was done by males and the meat they brought home had to be cut up, roasted, or hung out to dry. The females gathered plant material that also had to be prepared for eating. For example, Mongongo nuts must be cracked and roasted.

In terms of hours worked per week, the picture is as follows: the average man works 44.5 hours per week in total, earning just fewer than 500 kcal per hour. The time spent working (per week) is made up of 21.6 hours foraging, 7.5 hours repairing tools and weapons, and 15.4 hours work around the camp. The women earn 631 kcal per hour, working a 40.1 hour week. Their working time is made up of 12.6 hours foraging, 5.1 hours in repairs, and 22.4 hours work around the camp.[26]

Whether foraging or doing camp chores, the individual is working for payment that is delayed. The payment comes in the form of shared-out food. If the payment had come in the form of money, it would have to have been spent on that same shared-out food, because there is nothing else to buy. If we assume that individuals are free to choose how much work they do each day, then we can put on an economist's hat (adopt an economic outlook) and anticipate a trade-off between work and leisure. In other words, the individual values work because of the money (energy) it brings in, and values leisure time because of the enjoyment of rest and social intercourse involved. So there comes a point (the optimal point) where the individual gains the same satisfaction from work done as from leisure time, and is indifferent between the two. If more time had been spent on work or leisure, then less satisfaction would have resulted. Of course, if the rate of pay for work were higher, or the returns of leisure-time greater, then the optimal point would shift. In fact, the optimal point shifts systematically as the wage rate increases, and the (mathematically described) shape of this shift is called the **labour supply curve**.

The point here is that every hour of work deprives the worker of one hour of leisure. The worker on a high income sacrifices a large amount of money to obtain increased leisure time, whereas the worker on a low income sacrifices little. This type of analysis is used by economists to predict how working people will react to changes in wages. It is devised for application to a monetary economy. But the !Kung San had no money. Nevertheless, by substituting energy for money we obtain the same results. In other words, the San divided their time between work and leisure in the same way as do people with money. Moreover, they worked roughly the same hours per week as we do.[27]

On this basis, it is possible to construct a model of the economy of the !Kung San.[28] As we have seen (above), the San did not live a hand-to-mouth existence. Most of what the foragers brought back could not be eaten right away, but had to be processed. Mongongo nuts must be cracked and roasted. Meat was cooked, or cut into strips and hung up to dry. Just as in the case of animal foraging, the **handling time** should be taken into account. In terms of hours per week, the work load of men and women is as follows: the average man works a 44.5 hour week in total, earning just under 500 kcal h^{-1} (2 MJ h^{-1}). Women earn 631 kcal h^{-1} (2.64 MJ h^{-1}) working a 40.1 hour week. We can use these figures to calculate the notional wage earned by hunters and gatherers. The basal metabolic rate (BMR) for men is 1,400 kcal per day (5850 kJ), while the working requirement is 2,250 kcal per day (9405 kJ), which is 1.60 as a multiple of BMR. The MBMR (multiple of the BMR) is a convenient unit of comparison of individuals of different body-size. The energy requirement for a working woman is 1.59 MBMR, so the calorie requirement for working men and women is the same, when taken as the MBMR.

We can use these requirements to set up a preliminary model of the labour supply situation. In human economics, a worker divides the time available into time spent working and time spent at leisure. Every hour of work deprives the worker of one leisure hour. On this plot of daily hours of work against total income, we can represent **wage rates** as lines fanning out from the origin, as shown in Figure 2.7. The higher the wage rate, the greater the slope of the line. Assuming that a worker is free to choose the amount of work done each day, we can expect that there will be a trade-off between work and leisure, resulting in a set of indifference curves tangent to the wage rate lines. All points on a particular indifference curve have equal utility for the worker. The optimum number of working hours, at a particular wage rate, is given by the point on the line which

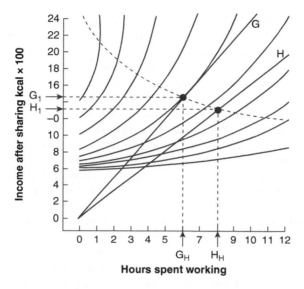

Figure 2.7 A simple economic model for San foraging. G is the wage rate for gathering, H is the wage rate for hunting

Note: For the full analysis of San economics in terms of energy (multiples of BMR), see McFarland (1989).

attains the greatest utility; that is the point at which the highest possible indifference curve is reached. By joining the optimum point on each wage rate line (by a dotted line) we attain the labour supply curve of human economic theory. Such curves have been obtained for people, using money as a measure of income, but they can also be obtained for animals, using energy as a measure of income.[29] Thus we are treating money and energy as equivalent, and taking foraging (earning energy) as synonymous with work (earning money).

There is quite a lot that we can say *a priori* about the labour supply situation in animals. First, there must be a sufficient income to sustain the BMR. So we can assume that an animal would be prepared to work nearly 24 hours a day at the lowest sustainable wage rate, otherwise it will die. There may be some animals willing to sacrifice their lives for some activity other than foraging, but these must operate above the minimal wage rate in order to have energy available for these other activities. Animals are able to go for long periods without food only when they have considerable unearned income to draw upon. Second, we can expect that there will always be a maximum income, earned or otherwise, beyond which the animal is simply not interested. We cannot expect to find animal millionaires who accumulate energy simply for the sake of it. The maximum income is that beyond which the animal derives no utility from further income. Third, we can assume that our animal will forage less when given free food, and this will alter the labour supply curve.

The San, like animals, are subject to similar metabolic constraints on their labour supply curve, and if we use a calorie scale of income, we obtain a picture something like that illustrated in Figure 2.7. We know from Lee[30] that 60% of the total calorie income comes from gathering wild plants. The average daily income is 2,355 kcal (9.84 MJ), so the average daily income from gathering is some 1,400 kcal (5.85 MJ), shown as wage rate G in Figure 2.7. The model indicates that it should take six hours per day to produce this income. A man-day of hunting brings in 7,230 kcal (30.2 MJ) on average, compared with 12,000 kcal (50.16 MJ) for a person-day of gathering. So the hunting wage rate (H) is only 60% of the gathering wage rate. On this basis, the model predicts an eight-hour day for hunting, with an income of about 1,250 kcal (5.23 MJ) after sharing. In fact, the women usually work a six hour day and the men an eight hour day, when foraging.[31]

These earnings are purely notional, in the sense that their value is dependent upon an exchange process. If there are many people in the camp, then the rate of exchange is low. If there are few, then the exchange rate is high. What a hunter or forager brings back from a particular day's work is of no direct benefit, because it is pooled with the produce from other foragers and shared out to all members of the group. It is as if the forager received a wage that is determined by the success of the company as a whole. In evolutionary terms, as we saw in Chapter 1, the San seem to be practising reciprocal altruism. Among humans in general, an altruistic act may take many forms, including baby minding, loan of tools, or a political favour. In advanced human societies it may be possible to quantify such favours in terms of money, but the San have no money. It seems likely that some forms of economic altruism existed before money was invented, and that money had its origins in exchange of favours.[32,33]

However, it appears that anthropologists and economists fail to agree about the origins of money. The "classical" story is that exchange amongst unrelated (non-kin) groups usually takes place at some kind of marketplace. In the absence of money, goods and services are bartered. There is bargaining between the opposing parties, each trying to maximize their profitability. If the barter exchanges are not direct, then some sort of accounts must be kept. There must be mutual trust, or some kind of policing. This type of barter market can work satisfactorily if relatively few commodities are involved in the exchange. A society that has some form of all-purpose money can operate a *price market*. The producers sell their goods in exchange for money, and use money to purchase other goods or services. The main advantage of a price market is that it can handle many commodities in a mixed economy. Another advantage is that it facilitates trade with strangers, with whom no elaborate trust arrangements exist. Traditionally, money has been regarded as a portable, recognizable material. It has a certain legality that makes it divisible and convertible, and confers wide generality of use.

This view is challenged by anthropologists on the grounds that barter is much more relaxed, less calculated, than it is often made out to be, and money is not a unitary (scalar quantity) as it is often made out to be. In other words, there are problems with classical microeconomics.

Problems with microeconomics

Microeconomics is a branch of economics concerned with the behaviour of individuals in making decisions about the allocation of limited resources. Typically, it applies to markets where goods and/or services are bought and sold. Decisions relating to supply and demand affect prices, and these determine the quantity supplied and quantity demanded of goods and services.[34]

We have seen that microeconomic principles can be applied to various animals, and hunter-gatherers, when prices are represented in terms of energy, rather than money. The problem is that such prices are taken to be scalar quantities, when in reality they are vector quantities. In the case of money, there is a face value, an exchange value, and an intrinsic value to be taken into account (see below).

In the case of energy, it has been convenient (e.g. optimal foraging theory[35]) to regard energy as a scalar quantity, but in reality it is nothing of the kind. We have seen (above) how foraging redshanks appear to maximize energy profitability some of the time, but in some circumstances they prefer to spend time taking less "profitable" prey. What redshanks gain from the prey is not only energy, but also essential nutrients. In other words what a foraging animal gains is not a unitary (scalar) quantity, but a complex (vector) quantity that will alter the animal's state in many ways.

The state of the animal can be represented as a point in a multidimensional space, and as the state changes it can be described as a trajectory in the state space.[36] Moreover, different points along the trajectory have different "costs" associated with them. This type of theoretical approach has been applied to a number of aspects of animal and robot behaviour,[37] but what interests us here is its application to nutrition.

Let us imagine a two-dimensional space in which an animal's requirement for carbohydrate and fat are represented by an internal target as shown in Figure 2.8. Only one type of food is available (this is often the case for domestic cats whose owners always provide the same commercial cat food). As the animal eats this food its state changes, and this change can be represented by a trajectory in the state space. The problem is that the trajectory does not allow the animal to reach its internal target, so the animal has to stop eating at the point on the trajectory that is nearest to the target. However there are various (mathematical) ways of determining the nearest point. Which mathematical rules should the animal adopt?

This type of problem is now called the "geometry of nutrition",[38] and it is currently regarded as a breakthrough in nutrition research, not only because of the elegant theory, but also because a wide variety of animals do behave in ways that conform to the theory. In fact the theory is now being applied to human nutrition,[39] and could well be relevant to microeconomics.

Consider the following scenario. In a two-dimensional space we can represent an individual's preferred state. This could be a nutritional state, or any kind of motivational state in which there is a target (preferred state). The individual can perform behaviour A, the consequences of which move the state along trajectory A, or behaviour B that results in trajectory B. Neither of these trajectories hit the target. Behaviours A and B can be deployed in a way that gets

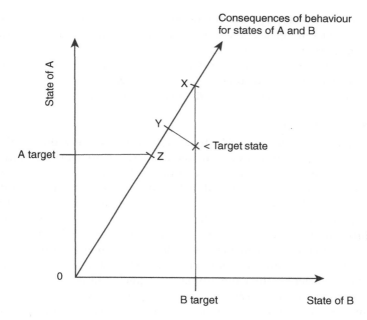

Figure 2.8 Imaginary two-dimensional state space in which the consequences of behaviour (e.g. eating a particular food) are represented

Note: Within the state space there is a target, but the consequences of behaviour cannot reach the target. The target state is bypassed by the trajectory representing the consequences of eating a particular food. Points X, Y and Z represent stopping places that are 'nearest' to the target state, but based upon different stopping rules.

as near as possible to the target. But what does "as near as possible" mean? It turns out that different species, even if closely related, have different rules that are tuned to their ecological situation.[40] In Figure 2.8, the three different stopping rules are illustrated. These rules have different effects on the elasticity of demand, even in a simplified two-dimensional situation. In a multidimensional situation these effects can be modelled using matrix algebra, sometimes with surprising results.[41]

The implications of the above scenario are relevant to cases where observed behaviour does not fit with standard microeconomic theory. Some of these apparent anomalies may be due to over-simplistic (scalar) representations of what is actually a multidimensional situation. It is difficult to portray a multidimensional space on a two-dimensional page, but the necessary matrix manipulations can be carried out on a computer, as has been demonstrated by the proponents of the geometry of nutrition.[42]

So far as conventional economics is concerned, there seems to be a *modelling problem,* in that scalar variables are sometimes used to represent what is really a multidimensional phenomenon.

Specific hungers

The term "specific hunger" stems from the discovery during the 1970s that most animals are unable to detect many essential nutrients (e.g. vitamins and minerals), either by taste or by their levels in the blood. Nevertheless, animals deficient in certain vitamins or minerals do develop strong preferences for foods containing the missing substances. For many years such specific hungers posed something of a problem for scientists trying to explain how animals knew which foods contained the beneficial ingredients. Eventually it turned out that if consumption of a novel food is followed by recovery from dietary deficiency, then the animal will quickly learn to prefer the novel food. Animals learn to avoid dangerous foods and to consume beneficial foods on the basis of general sensations of sickness or health.[43]

Here we are taking the liberty of extending the role of specific hungers beyond the area of nutrition, and into the realm of metaphorical hungers, for sex, status, and so on. As an example, let us consider this account[44] of the Gunwinggu people of Australia. Two tribes get together to exchange goods, on the basis of what anthropologists call **spheres of exchange**, in which certain types of good are considered to be equivalent, such as cloth for spears. A certain amount of dancing and feasting goes on, including what is called *dzamalog exchange.* This is a form of temporary swapping of women between the two tribes that may never meet again. In such situations, the currency of exchange is not simply material goods, but also some sex. Biologically, this is an example of **exogamy**, or outbreeding. Without some exogamy small tribes would be in danger of inbreeding, with all its deleterious consequences.[45]

From the point of view of the "trader" the "market" is a place where there is a multidimensional payoff. In other words, the trader has a "specific hunger" for certain goods, such as cloth or spears, but also a specific hunger (albeit subliminal) for sexual exchange. In other words, and contrary to standard microeconomic practice, the goods gained (e.g. food, sex) and the price paid (e.g. goods, time, tokens) are not scalar quantities, but vector quantities. In the next chapter we can see what a difference this view might make.

Points to remember

- Animals can be assumed to make rational decisions in the sense that their choices are consistent and transitive.
- There are analogies between human consumer economics and the costs and benefits incurred by animals. Money is analogous to energy, and utility is analogous to benefit (increment in fitness). Time and energy budgets can be analysed on this basis.
- Regarding the outcome of economic behaviour in terms of a single scalar variable (e.g. money) can be an oversimplification.

Further reading

Cuthill, I.C. and Houston, A.I. (1997) Managing time and energy. In Krebs, J.R. and Davies, N.B. (eds) *Behavioural Ecology*, 4th edn. Blackwell, Oxford.

Heinrich, B. (1979) *Bumblebee Economics*. Harvard University Press, Cambridge, MA.

Kacelnik, A. (2006) Meanings of rationality. In Hurley, S. and Nudds, M. (eds) *Rational Animals*. Oxford University Press, Oxford.

McFarland, D. (1989) Economic Altruism. In *Problems of Animal Behaviour*, pp. 59–80. Longman, London and Wiley, New York.

McFarland, D.J. and Houston, A.I. (1981) *Quantitative Ethology: The State Space Approach*. Pitman, London.

Stephens, D.W. and Krebs, J.R. (1986) *Foraging Theory*. Princeton University Press, Princeton, NJ.

Essential reading (for the modelling problem)

Simpson, S.J. and Raubenheimer, D. (2007) A multi-level analysis of feeding behaviour. The geometry of nutrition. *Proc. R. Soc. Lond. B. Biol. Sci.*, 62A, 707–713.

3
Behavioural Economics

In the mid-20th century psychologists in the developing field of cognitive psychology, such as Ward Edwards,[1] Amos Tversky, and Daniel Kahneman began to compare their cognitive models of decision-making under risk and uncertainty with economic models of rational behaviour. In 1979, Kahneman and Tversky[2] wrote an important paper that used cognitive psychology to explain various divergences of economic decision-making from neo-classical theory. They were the founders of prospect theory.

Prospect theory has two stages, an editing stage and an evaluation stage. In the editing stage, the subject simplifies the situation, using various choice **heuristics**. At the evaluation stage, risky alternatives are evaluated in terms of psychological principles, such as reference dependence, loss aversion, probability weighting functions, and diminishing sensitivity to gains and losses.[3]

Prospect theory could account for a number of anomalies in pre-existing theory (such as expected utility theory and rank dependent utility). In 1992, Tversky and Kahneman[4] produced a revised version of prospect theory, called cumulative prospect theory, that allowed for non-linear probability weighting in a cumulative manner. In 2002, Daniel Kahneman received the Nobel Prize in Economics for his work on prospect theory (Amos Tversky was no longer alive).

Amos Tversky and his collaborators showed that classical economic rationality is systematically violated, and that decision-making errors are both widespread and predictable. In the early 1970s, Tversky and Kahneman published a ground-breaking series of papers that focused on judgements about the likelihood of uncertain events. (This work is summarized in a 1974 *Science* article, "Judgement under uncertainty: heuristics and biases", whose dramatic impact has spread across the social sciences.) They argued that people rely on a limited number of heuristic principles to simplify complex probability judgements. They documented many decision-making anomalies that can be traced to three simple decision-making short-cuts (called representativeness, availability, and anchoring).[5]

Some critics of behavioural economics complain that experimentally observed behaviour has limited application in the real world. The early experiments were conducted in a traditional experimental psychology setting (i.e. in a laboratory free of "distractions"). In later experiments subjects were asked about their preferences.

In this chapter we take a look at these issues from a biological viewpoint. Firstly, to what extent are experiments on economic behaviour that are conducted in a laboratory representative of real life? Secondly, Tversky and Kahneman accounted for their experimental results in psychological terms; we consider the implications of the fact that similar phenomena occur in a variety of animals, for which human psychological terminology is not appropriate.

The experimental situation

Many of the experimental studies of human economic behaviour take place in an environment that is not really comparable to that of the real world. Take, for example, the following advertisement.

Welcome!

The **Lab for Experimental Economics & Decision Research** (LEEDR) was established in 1996 in the Department of Applied Economics & Management at Cornell University. As a national leader, researchers have used LEEDR to study a wide variety of economic and psychological phenomena, including behavioural anomalies in public goods, the efficiency of energy markets, charitable giving, the funding of commodity advertising, the causes of obesity, and the impacts of stigma. The facility is dedicated to research and consists of 24 subject computers equipped with privacy shields, two monitor computers, and the latest in audio and visual equipment.

Experiments conducted in such an environment lack the complexity, not to say the distractions, typical of the situations in which ordinary people make economic decisions. However, the same can be said of the early investigations of the economic behaviour of non-human subjects. These were performed on rats and pigeons in the laboratory (see below for further details). The results obtained were similar to those typical of human "rational" economic behaviour.[6] Such studies have their critics and defenders.[7] But from a biological viewpoint, what matters is the behaviour of animals in an unnatural environment.

The sterile environment

Experimentally observed behaviour usually takes place in a standardized environment. For the results of such experiments to be verified, it must be possible for experiments to be repeated in a situation that is comparable to the original. In the 20th century, an apparatus called the Skinner box was widely used in behavioural psychology as an experimental tool. The apparatus is named after its inventor, the psychologist B.F. Skinner. For many decades the Skinner box was used by experimental psychologists in investigating animal learning and other aspects of behaviour, but over time some experimenters began to realize that there were various peculiar anomalies associated with this type of apparatus.

A Skinner box is a chamber that contains a device (usually a bar or key) that an animal can press or manipulate in order to obtain food or water as a type of reinforcement. The box also has a device that records each response provided by the animal. During experiments in a Skinner box the animal is rewarded for performing a particular act (e.g. pigeons peck at an illuminated key, rats press a bar to obtain access to food/water, etc.). Their behaviour is automatically reinforced by means of a specified reinforcement schedule. This reinforcement occurs in particular stimulus situation (the Skinner box), and certain features of the stimulus situation will inevitably become associated with reinforcement, thus providing the essential conditions for **classical conditioning**. This happens because the reinforcer used in an experiment is also a potential unconditional stimulus (UCS) that will automatically elicit an innate set of responses. In chickens, these responses include scratching for food, and in pigs, rooting behaviour.

In many cases the responses are not really arbitrary, but part of the repertoire of instinctive behaviour that normally is associated with the reward. If this interpretation is correct, then we might expect that pigeons pecking a key for a food reward would do so in a manner different from that employed when they are working for water reward. Examination of a film of pigeons during key-pecking behaviour shows that this is in fact the case. When students were asked to distinguish between filmed food and water test sessions, without knowing which reinforcer was being used, they were able to judge with 87% accuracy.[8] Birds pecking for food strike the key with an open beak using sharp, vigorous pecks. When pecking for water, the bill remains closed and contact with the key is more sustained. Water pecking is often accompanied by the pumping (swallowing) movements typical of pigeon drinking behaviour (unlike other birds, pigeons drink by sucking up the water).

If pigeons are exposed to repeated pairings of key illumination and food presentation, they will begin to peck the key without any training. If the lighted key is paired with grain, and the pigeons peck the key as if it were grain, as a result of straightforward Pavlovian conditioning. The point can be demonstrated even more clearly if the key illumination is paired with a reinforcement to which pecking is not the pigeons' natural response. This can be done by offering the pigeons a sexual reward. Paired male and female pigeons are housed in adjacent chambers separated by a sliding door. Once a day, the stimulus light is turned on and the sliding door is removed so the male can begin his courtship display. Within five to 10 trials, the males begin to make conditioned responses towards the stimulus light. The pigeons direct their courtship towards the light, thus behaving towards it as if it were a female.[9] This phenomenon is called **autoshaping**.[10]

To prevent a pigeon from obtaining any instrumental reinforcement during an autoshaping experiment, it is possible to arrange matters so that the food reward is withheld whenever the pigeon pecks the key. Under these conditions, autoshaped pigeons persist in pecking; such is the strength of the Pavlovian conditioning.[11] These and other autoshaping procedures have established beyond doubt that complex behaviour patterns such as feeding, drinking, and courtship can be established by means of Pavlovian conditioning. Modern behavioural economics experiments often take place in the equivalent of a Skinner box. In such a situation, the subjects of repeated experiments will be likely to develop anomalies involving autoshaping. In other words, the person in the testing situation is likely to become conditioned (autoshaping does occur in humans) to stimuli that are basically irrelevant to the task in hand.

Now let us consider a different type of anomaly. If hungry doves are allowed to work for food in a Skinner box until they are satiated, their work rate declines exponentially. Close examination of their behaviour shows that they peck at a constant rate, but intersperse pecking with pauses in such a way that their overall rate of working declines exponentially. If a hungry dove is fitted with paper clips on its wing feathers, it may attempt to remove the clips during the characteristic pauses in feeding. Similarly, if a hungry dove is allowed to peck one key for food and another for water, it may fill in some of the feeding pauses by pecking for water. In other words the system controlling feeding behaviour is allocating time for other activities. In doves, this may have to do with a trade-off between feeding and vigilance, since in nature a dove feeds in situations where there might be predators. However, this *time-sharing* phenomenon is found in many species of mammal, bird, and fish, in many types of situations.[12] Theoretical work suggests that animals follow an optimal path (i.e. an optimal behaviour sequence) in situations where they have "many things to do".[13]

The point to be made here is that an animal in a sterile environment does not behave "rationally". It does not "get on with the job" in the most efficient manner, nor does it behave as it would in the natural environment, because it is a captive in a laboratory environment.

The captive animal

Wild animals in captivity do not behave normally. They do not have to work for their food. They do not have predators. Their sex lives are determined by outsiders. They have time on their hands. In the real world, most animals have species-typical daily routines. They experience changes in environmental conditions between night and day, which affect them both directly and indirectly. These may include changes in food availability, and in numbers of predators, which are brought about by changes in temperature, light intensity, and so on.

In adjusting to the differences between night and day the animal adopts a daily routine which is made up of many different aspects of behaviour fitted together to form a pattern that tends to be repeated day after day, albeit changing with the seasons.

The most important daily changes in the external environment are those of light intensity and temperature. Animals specialized for daytime vision may be disadvantaged at night, because they are vulnerable to predators, or because they cannot forage efficiently. In cold climates it can benefit small mammals to be active at night when temperatures are low. Their period of greatest heat production then occurs during the coldest part of the 24-hour cycle, the activity being harnessed as a means of thermoregulation. Small birds, on the other hand, save energy on cold nights by becoming inactive and allowing their body temperature to fall. In hot climates it is advantageous for small mammals to be nocturnal and so avoid the heat of the day.

It is not surprising that rhythms of rest and activity are widespread in the animal kingdom. When it is disadvantageous to be active at night, the best policy is to sit tight in a safe place and save as much energy as possible. This has been suggested as one of the prime functions of sleep.[14] Nocturnal species may hide during the day if they are likely to be preyed upon. If they are themselves nocturnal predators, they may remain hidden and inactive during the day to avoid scaring their prey. Thus the daily rhythms of the physical environment make some activities advantageous at one time and disadvantageous at another. Much depends upon the overall ecology of the species concerned. Humans have characteristic daily routines, typically sleeping in a safe place at night for about eight hours, and spending eight hour working and eight hours cooking and socializing.[15]

An animal which is adapted to its environment will settle into a daily routine designed to maximize the survival value of its various activities. This is partly a matter of making the most of opportunities. For example, the European kestrel is a diurnal predator which specializes in preying upon small mammals. The bird relies on vision to detect and catch its prey and hunts most successfully when the light is good. Field studies reveal that kestrels catch prey throughout the day but do not always immediately eat what they catch. They tend to cache surplus prey in randomly chosen locations in their hunting area. The caching occurs throughout the day and the cached items are typically retrieved at dusk. This routine enables the kestrel to make the most of the available prey during the day, without spending too much time eating the prey. Moreover, if the bird ate all its surplus prey immediately it would become unnecessarily heavy and its hunting efficiency would probably decline. In addition to the daily routines typical of their own species, individual animals may develop their own daily habits. Thus kestrels that have found food at a particular time and place tend to repeat the same search pattern the next day. Such a strategy is appropriate in circumstances where the prey also has its own typical daily routine.

In captivity, animal behaviour is abnormal. Not only is the animal unable to engage in certain activities, it also has too much time on its hands. Technically it is in **limbo**.[16] Animals in such conditions often exhibit abnormal behaviour, especially **stereotypy**, which is repetitive behaviour in captive animals, particularly those given inadequate mental stimulation. Such behaviour may be maladaptive, involving self-injury or reduced reproductive success, and in laboratory animals can confound behavioural research.[17]

Many stereotypies can be induced by confinement; for example, cats pace in zoo cages.[18] Pregnant sows whose feed is restricted bite at their stalls' bars and chew without anything in their mouths.[19] Examples of stereotypical behaviours include pacing, rocking, swimming in circles, excessive sleeping, self-mutilation (including feather picking and excessive grooming), and mouthing cage bars. Stereotypies are seen in many species, including primates, carnivores, herbivores, and birds. Stereotypical behaviours are thought to be caused ultimately by artificial environments that do not allow animals to satisfy their normal behavioural needs. Rather than refer to the behaviour as abnormal, it has been suggested that it be described as behaviour indicative of an abnormal environment.

In summary, behaviour that occurs in a sterile environment is likely to be abnormal, in three main ways: classical conditioning to stimuli (autoshaping); sub-optimal behaviour sequences (time-sharing); stereotyped behaviour. Much of the research in behavioural economics occurs in a sterile environment, and it would be interesting to know how such environments affect human judgement and performance.

The real world

In the real world, the time allocated to various activities depends partly upon internal biological clocks, and partly upon the opportunities, advertised or otherwise, that present themselves in the form of external stimuli.[20] Often, the animal will have alternative, mutually exclusive possible courses of action, and will have to decide which to pursue. Unlike the sterile laboratory or cage, the real world is complex.

Animals in the real world

Let us start by looking at a study of animal economics in the real world. A female herring gull lays three eggs in a shallow nest on the ground, usually in a large breeding colony. Normally, the female and male take turns incubating, and they cover the eggs 98% of the time during the four-week incubation period. A sitting bird will not leave the nest until relieved by its partner, unless it is flushed out by a predator. Usually the partner leaves the nest to forage for food for a few hours. Sometimes, however, the partner's return may be delayed as a result of some mishap. What then happens? What should the sitting bird do? Its partner may return at any time, but on the other hand the sitting bird becomes increasingly hungry as time passes. Eventually the sitting bird should quit the nest and search for food, even though this means that the eggs will almost certainly be lost to a predator or marauding neighbours. Herring gulls breed for many successive years, and it is not in the genetic interests of the individual to endanger its life for a clutch of eggs, which are likely to produce only one fledgling if any; or which has only a 27% chance of producing one fledgling.

To investigate this question, we need to know (among other things) the cost of not sitting on the eggs. That is, we need to measure the risk to the eggs of being left unattended and the risk to the bird of being without food. Rudi Drent[21] measured the risk to the eggs due to exposure to the weather. He found that, in the absence of the parent, the embryo risks death from either overheating or chilling. However, a more important factor is the total amount of heat supplied by the time the hatching date arrives. The rate of development of the embryo depends on its metabolism, which in turn is affected by the temperature inside the egg. During incubation the egg gradually loses weight as a result of water evaporation. This loss of water results in an air space at one end of the egg, necessary for the embryo to breath during the period shortly before hatching. The embryo must not develop too quickly or the air space will not be formed properly by the time it is ready to hatch. It must not develop too slowly, or the egg will have lost so much water that the embryo will become dehydrated. Hatching must occur when only a certain amount of water has been lost from the egg, and when the embryo has received enough heat to be ready to hatch. Thus two parallel processes must reach their critical points simultaneously. Normally, the eggs can survive the climatic exposure that occurs when birds are forced to leave the nest by a predator. However, if the birds are disturbed repeatedly, the average supply of heat may fall short of that required for successful hatching.

A herring gull egg is about twice as likely to be lost through predation as from failure to develop properly. The risk to an egg can be estimated by experiments in which the parents are removed from the nest. The results of one such study[22] show a half-life of about eight hours. The risk to a sitting bird of being without food can also be investigated experimentally. For example, the bodyweight of an incubating bird can be measured by placing a specially designed balance under the nest. The amount of fat that the animal is carrying can be calculated from its weight in relation to its skeletal size (measured when the bird is initially caught and marked). The amount of food that a herring gull obtains from foraging can be estimated from the change in weight measured on the nest balance before and after foraging trips. The quality of the food can be estimated from analysis of the faecal remains gathered from around the nest, and from observations made of the bird while foraging. Herring gulls may fly a number of miles while foraging; to obtain observations on foraging, particular birds were fitted with radio transmitters and tracked by means of a directional radio receiver. Thus by using a variety of experimental techniques, it is sometimes possible to arrive at a fairly accurate picture of the costs and benefits incurred by animals living a normal life in a natural environment. Such experimental studies are designed to investigate the actual risks, costs, and benefits incurred in the working environment. In this particular case, Richard Sibly and Robin McCleery[23] were interested in modelling the total economy of herring gulls during the incubation period. Their aim was to investigate the pros and cons of the possible alternatives in terms of biological fitness. They found that the feeding preferences of individual gulls were very important determinants of fitness. They constructed a fitness landscape for each breeding pair (an example is shown in Figure 3.1) based upon two important hunger variables which they called the *normal feeding threshold* and the *desperation feeding threshold*. The former is the degree of hunger at which a bird would leave its territory to forage if one of

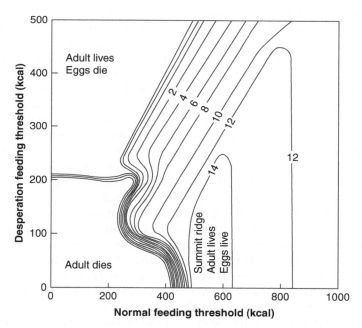

Figure 3.1 A selective landscape with desperation feeding threshold and normal feeding threshold as axes. The lines represent contours of equal fitness. There are three main features of this landscape. Maximum fitness is attained along the "summit ridge", where the adult lives and the eggs hatch. To the right of the ridge, fitness declines because of the cost of carrying extra weight. Minimum fitness occurs when the adult dies. On the plateau at top left, the adult lives but the eggs die
Source: From Sibly and McCleery (1983).

its preferred foods became available, provided that its partner was present to take over incubation (mated pairs usually have different preferred foods that are available at different periods of time, or of the tidal cycle). The latter is the degree of hunger at which the bird would leave its nest to feed, even if its mate was not available for incubation duty. On the basis of the fitness calculations they identified various characteristics of the optimal behaviour strategies.

In particular, (1) they predicted that energy reserves should be maintained between 500 and 1,200 kcal; (2) that members of a mated pair should have complementary food preferences, at least one of these being a preference for feeding at the local rubbish tip, where food is available only at specific tipping times each day, not including Saturday and Sunday; and (3) that a parent should desert its offspring if its energy reserves fall below 200 kcal. They were able to test these predictions by observation and experiment. This is an example of animal economic activity studied in the field, and there have been many since.[24] Many such studies evaluate the situation in terms of some index of fitness, and this raises the question of proximal causes. In this particular case, the two parents have to cooperate, and this is done by means of a fairly elaborate signalling system.[25] In addition, the foraging gull is very sensitive to the time of day and the state of the tide. For example, those foraging at the local rubbish tip would turn up in large numbers at the times when the trucks were due, having finished their morning, or afternoon, collections. The gulls did not turn up at weekends, but they did turn up on Bank Holiday Mondays, only to be disappointed. Thus the gulls, like most other animals, make the most of their opportunities, but they also have to cope with risks, of losing an investment (e.g. eggs), of starvation, and of predation. The incubating herring gull faces many risks and uncertainties. Are they sensitive to such risks, or are they merely automata?

Alex Kacelnic and Melissa Bateson[26] note that a number of different fields of behavioural research have converged on the problem of how animals respond to risk. They reviewed some 59 experimental studies of risk sensitivity in animals that are based upon the normative risk-sensitivity theory (RST). They also reviewed descriptive models and note that these and the RST models make no effort to suggest how such behaviour might be implemented by a plausible information-processing system. On the other hand, process-based models based on associative learning theory, and models based upon scalar expectancy theory do posit some kind of mechanism. Their overall conclusion at the time of writing (1997) was that the four theories are complementary in the sense that: "We do not believe that any of these approaches substitutes for any other: all can contribute to a full understanding of risk sensitivity". The point to be made here is that risk sensitivity in non-human animals is an active field of research. Over the past two decades biologists have researched this phenomenon,[27] and while they may not always agree about details the general conclusion is unequivocal. Risk sensitivity is widespread in the animal kingdom, a fact that the psychological theorizing typical of behavioural economics may find hard to explain.

Humans in the real world

In the real world night follows day with regularity, and there are consequently dangers and opportunities of economic importance. All animals on this planet are subject to this circadian variation, humans included. Each animal species is adapted to the circadian cycle, some diurnal (e.g. hawks), others nocturnal (e.g. owls). Humans are fundamentally diurnal, and although there are night-workers in the industrial world, prolonged night-work is damaging to human health.[28] Once humans became settled rather than nomadic, there were economic costs associated with safety at night.[29] In evolutionary terms, humans had time and energy at their disposal, but it was the novel uses of energy that transformed the human lifestyle. Early humans made fires, wore animal skins, and (later) domesticated animals and built dwellings.

Some hunter-gatherer groups have been studied in terms of their use of time and energy, in a way that is similar to animal studies,[30] and one way to measure the evolution of human economic activity is to look at *energy capture*. To function efficiently, the adult human body requires about 2,000 kcal of food per day. Prior to the Neolithic revolution humans, captured energy by making fires and wearing animal skins, and thus captured about 3,000 kcal. With the domestication of animals, this figure climbed to about 5,000 kcal. In 1971, the geoscientist Earl Cook[31] compiled a graph of the energy capture per person up to modern times, and his calculations have stood the tests of time. Hunter-gatherers capture about 2–4 kcal per person per day; early agriculturalists about 12 kcal; advanced agriculturalists about 30 kcal; those living in an industrial society about 77 kcal, and those living in a technological society about 230 kcal per day.

Using energy to devise a way of producing (e.g. making a fire) or saving (e.g. making clothes) energy is an aspect of **ultra-sociality**, as a result of which individuals are able to harness much more energy than they would as a product of normal social evolution. This is a phenomenon that humans share with some social insects.[32]

Using energy to create a store of energy (e.g. food) involves a risk that the energy invested may be lost. Fundamentally, all economic activity boils down to the use of time and energy. Time cannot be stored, but energy can. Hoarded food, stored fuel, and stored "tokens" with which to exchange hoarded items are the basic economic units. In addition to the risks associated with a particular activity, there are risks associated with being in a particular state. Every species has limited **tolerance** of environmental factors such as temperature. In other words the animal's (multidimensional) physiological state is bounded by lethal limits. As the animal's state approaches a lethal boundary there is an increasing probability that the boundary will be crossed.[33] In other words, there is an increasing risk associated with that state. Similarly, there is a risk associated with hoarded food, hoarded goods, or hoarded money.

Hoarding and caching

Hoarding and caching are interchangeable terms, although hoarding is used more in relation to mammals, while caching is common in the bird literature. Hoarding by animals involves the storage of food in locations hidden from the sight of both conspecifics and members of other species.[34] Most commonly, the function of hoarding is to store food in times of surplus for times when food is less plentiful. Hoarding is done either on a long-term basis, on a seasonal cycle, with food to be consumed months down the line – or on a short term basis, in which case the food will be consumed over a period of one or several days. There is evidence that some amount of caching is done in order to ripen the food, called ripening caching. Some common animals that cache their food are rodents such as squirrels and hamsters; many bird species also do it, including rooks and woodpeckers. There are two types of caching behaviour: larder-hoarding, where a species creates a few large caches which it often defends; and scatter-hoarding, where a species creates multiple caches, often with each individual food item stored in a special place.

Caching is a common response to seasonal changes in food availability. In regions where winters are harsh, food availability typically becomes low, and caching food during the times of high food availability in the warmer months provides a significant survival advantage. However, in *ripening caching* behaviour, animals collect and cache food which is inedible at the time but will become "ripe" and edible after a short while. For instance, alligators are predators with limited tooth action – they can bite prey to kill it but can't tear flesh or chew. Small enough prey are swallowed whole, while the carcass of larger prey, such as a deer, is cached underwater and left to rot until it becomes edible. Leafcutter ants harvest pieces of inedible leaves and then cache them in underground chambers to ripen with a fungus, thus providing the main food for the colony.

Nomadic human hunter-gatherers could not hoard food, and it has been argued that there are two different kinds of food-gathering societies, because there are two radically distinct types of economy.[35] The first is found among nomadic hunter-gatherers such as the Bushmen (San) and the Australian aborigines. It is based on the immediate use of food resources. This economy is flexible and relies on multiple alternative strategies. The second is found among more sedentary foragers, such as the Northwest Coast and California Indians. This is based on large-scale seasonal food storage.

Nomadic hunter-gatherers move from one site to another according to seasonal fluctuations in food resources. Group migrations usually follow natural rhythms, often reproducing those of previous years. In this way such people avoid the necessity of storing food. In the case of the storing hunter-gatherer economy, where natural food resources are bountiful, but seasonal, they can be gathered while available and stored. Such a system depends upon appropriate food-preservation techniques.

In the developed world (i.e. post-Neolithic revolution) storage is an important factor. As we have seen, some animals store food, and sometimes other materials. However, nomadic hunter-gatherer humans could not store anything that was not easily transportable. With the arrival of the Neolithic revolution, which started in different places at different times (and in some places never started, the inhabitants remaining hunter-gatherers until very recently), there was a large increase in the human population and reproductive success, but the lifespan of most individuals was reduced. This reduction was partly due to excessive consumption of foods to which the people were not evolutionarily adjusted, and partly to changes in lifestyle, such as living in one place. Nomadic peoples move on, and to some extent leave their enemies behind. The longer you stay in one place the more you attract rats and mice, and other disease-bearing creatures. The more you stay in one place, the more the population increases, and the greater the chance of cross-infection. The advantages of staying in one place are that pottery can be made and used for more efficient cooking. Food can be stored against lean times, and various community activities can develop.

The ability to store food for the winter was a necessity for humans inhabiting cold climates, but it was not that difficult and relatively risk-free. Food storage is warmer climates carried considerable risk. As we saw in Chapter 1, the evidence suggests that farmers suffered higher rates of infection due to the increase in the size and permanence of human settlements, poorer nutrition due to reduced meat intake, and greater interference with mineral absorption due to the cereal-based diet. Consequently, Neolithic farmers were shorter and had a lower life expectancy relative to their hunter-gatherer ancestors. However there was a rise in the birth rate and a large population increase.

Before the Neolithic period, all animal foods consumed by humans were derived from wild animals. The absolute quantity of fat in wild mammals is dependent on the species, but (apart from marine mammals) the wild animal carries much less fat than its domesticated counterpart. Moreover the type of fat found in wild animals is less deleterious for the human diet.[36] So the early years of storage in the form of plant material and domesticated animals had a profound deleterious effect upon the lifestyle of the individual.

In modern economies, hoarding is the practice of obtaining and holding scarce resources, possibly so that they can be sold to customers for profit, but also, sometimes, in response to fear of social disruption, or fear of a shortage of some good. Civil unrest or natural disaster may lead people to collect foodstuffs, water, fuel, or other essentials which they believe, rightly or wrongly, will soon be in short supply.

Compulsive hoarding or hoarding disorder is a pattern of behaviour that is now regarded as a mental disorder[37] manifested in 2–5% of adults, and often presenting before the age of 21. Family histories show strong positive correlations, and the onset is often correlated with stressful life events.[38] Compulsive hoarding can take many forms, including collecting cooking pots, furniture, pottery, and books that are never read. Extensive hoarding often interferes with the lifestyle of the household, can be an economic burden, and can increase the risk of fire, poor sanitation, and health-threatening conditions. Compulsive hoarders do not include those who hoard money, even though some individuals hoard more than a hundred times more money than they could possibly spend during their life.

Hoarding items removes them from general circulation, and this can cause social problems. This is especially true of money and food. Anthropologically, hoarding is supposed to benefit the community as a whole, but in the modern world this is not always the case.[39]

The rationality muddle

We now come to a fundamental question that divides biologists from most other disciplines. In ordinary language, we think of rationality as a feature of thinking people that they exhibit when they adopt beliefs on the basis of appropriate reasons. Rationality can be contrasted with non-rationality and irrationality. A stone is non-rational because it is not capable of carrying out rational assessments. A person that is capable being rational, but who nevertheless violates the principles of rational assessment, is being irrational. The philosopher Fred Dretske[40] distinguishes between minimal rationality, doing something for reasons, and normative rationality – doing something for good reasons. The drunken man looking for his keys under a lamp post – not because he left them there, but because the light is better there – is demonstrating minimal rationality.

A rational person is expected to be coherent, responsive, and self-critical. Thus a person holds beliefs irrationally if any one belief conflicts with any other, if their beliefs are not adapted in the face of contrary evidence, or if their assumptions are not open to question. In everyday life, a rational person does not have to subject each and every belief to constant conscious deliberation. He or she may hold beliefs intuitively, through habit, or on some authority. However, a rational person must be able to muster a good defence of a belief, when the occasion demands. A belief contrary to the dictates of reason is irrational. Some beliefs, however, are non-rational because they are matters of taste, and no reasons are required (I prefer the colour blue, but many small girls prefer pink). Similarly, some beliefs are non-rational because they are necessarily matters of faith; some people have a religious faith, whereas I have a materialist faith (i.e. I believe that all aspects of the universe, including all our thoughts and feelings are, in principle, explainable in material terms. Note that such materialism is still a matter of faith). Ingrained emotional responses, such as certain phobias (e.g. of height, or of spiders), are also non-rational.

Rational thought does not always result in rational behaviour. A person may know what behaviour is rational, but may be compelled, or may choose, to opt for behaviour which is not rational. Normally we think of a rational person as being capable of performing a number of actions, and of knowing the consequences of each, and having a complete and consistent order of preference among them. We can also expect a rational person to solve certain types of problem, such as the transitive inference problem. Suppose we tell a person that A is bigger than B, and that B is bigger than C, and then ask whether C is smaller than A. We would expect them to be able to infer, from the information provided, that C is smaller than A. If a person was unable to deal with such a problem, or was inconsistent in answering such questions, we would conclude that they were being non-rational (e.g. not paying attention), or irrational.

At one time it was thought that a capability for rational thought was necessary for solving such transitive inference problems. But it is now known that young children, squirrel monkeys, and even pigeons can master such problems.[41] The evidence suggests that either such participants are capable of cognitive reasoning, or that there is some seat-of-the-pants, non-cognitive ability to order things transitively, which can be revealed by well-designed experiments. It is not for us to enter into this academic minefield,[42] but we can note that a rational decision-maker is one that consistently makes the same choice when in the same state and when given the same set of options. This implies that the options can be ordered with respect to one another, and that the first option in the ranking is always the one chosen, and that multiple choices are transitive. Moreover, the choices are made in accordance with some maximization principle (always choose the top option in the ranking). In other words, the rational decision-maker maximizes some quantity. In economics, this quantity is called *utility*.

Utility is a notional measure of the psychological value of goods, leisure, and so on. It is a notional measure because we do not know (in scientific terms) how it influences choice behaviour, but economists assume that utility is maximized by a rational decision-maker. Let us look at a classical economics textbook.[43]

> *The law of diminishing marginal utility.* As you consume more of the same good, your total (psychological) utility increases. However, let us use the term marginal utility to refer to "the extra utility added by one extra last unit of the good". Then, with successive new units of the good, your total utility will grow at a slower and slower rate because of a fundamental tendency for your psychological ability to appreciate more of the good to become less keen. This fact, that the increments in total utility fall off, economists describe as follows: As the amount consumed of a good increases, the *marginal utility* of the good (or the extra utility added by its last unit) tends to decrease.

To a biologist this is an extraordinary statement. Firstly, the idea that the phenomenon is associated with some kind of "psychological ability" is pure surmise. Secondly, the phenomenon named "diminishing marginal utility" is widespread throughout the animal kingdom. It has been described in many ways, including feedback control theory and optimality theory.[44] These approaches make no assumptions as to the "psychological or physiological" mechanisms involved. As we shall see in Chapter 4, some of the assumptions about the mechanisms involved in economic decision-making may prove to be valid, but the subject is very controversial, and the jury is out and will probably remain out for a very long time.

Rational choice theory

Rational choice theory, widely used in microeconomic studies, simply assumes that choices are made in a consistent manner, ranking the choice alternatives. There are no assumptions as to the mechanisms employed. The corollary of this approach is that choices are transitive, and this implies that some quantity is maximized. This approach to rationality is virtually a tautology. Nevertheless, investigations can be carried out to see whether people's choices are consistent with this view. In recent years the theoretical vision of rational choice theory has become more and more clouded by the experimental results of behavioural economics. So, overall, it seems that human choice behaviour does not conform to the theory, and the theory has come in for a lot of criticism.[45]

The evolutionary psychology perspective suggests that many of the seeming contradictions and biases regarding rational choice can be explained as being rational in the context of maximizing biological fitness in the ancestral environment but not necessarily in the modern one. Thus, when living at subsistence level where a reduction of resources may have meant death it may have been rational to place a greater value on losses than on gains. It may also explain differences between groups such as males being less risk-averse than females. The males, after all, usually have a more hazardous (hunting) lifestyle. While unsuccessful risk-seeking may limit reproductive success for both sexes, males may potentially increase their reproductive success much more than females from successful risk-seeking. Of interest from this viewpoint is the situation with other species.

Biological rationality

The notion of rationality arises in a variety of disciplines. Philosophers and psychologists regard a rational process as one where beliefs, actions, and so on, are adopted for appropriate reasons. This type of rationality has been dubbed "philosophical or psychological rationality" (P-rationality).[46] Economists regard behaviour as rational when it maximizes a quantity (usually some kind of *utility*) no matter what process produces the behaviour (E-rationality). Biologists are interested in principles of maximization that relate to fitness (B-rationality).

Whereas P-rationality refers to a process, E-rationality and B-rationality relate to behavioural outcomes. Thus if I see my dog catching and eating a mouse, I can ask whether a rational process is involved (P-rationality), whether the dog is behaving efficiently and economically (E-rationality), or whether the dog is improving its genetic fitness (B-rationality). If the dog catches the mouse in an unthinking reflex manner, then the first answer is no. If the dog catches the mouse with speed and skill, and little energy expenditure, then the second answer might be yes. If the dog eats the mouse and is subsequently ill, then the third answer might be no.[47] Although transitivity of choice has been demonstrated in many animal species, it is not always straightforward. Let us take the hummingbird as an example. Observations by Hurly and Oseen, made during field studies of risk preference by wild rufous hummingbirds (*Selasphorus rufus*), have shown apparent violations of E-rationality, namely preference reversals due to context.[48]

Wild, free-living hummingbirds were given choices between artificial flowers that differed in the level of variance in the amount of sugar solution they contained. Three types of flowers were identified by their colour. Type N (no variance) always contained the same amount of sugar; Type M (medium variance) provided a coefficient of variation of 33.3%; Type H (high variance) offered a coefficient of variation of 66.6%. The hummingbirds significantly preferred N over M and N over H, when offered the alternatives in pairs. However, when the birds were presented with the three types of flowers simultaneously, their preference was for M (medium variance). Similar results have come from studies of other species, including honeybees, jays, and starlings.[49] Various explanations have been offered for this type of result.[50] An economist might well conclude that such animals are simply being irrational, but a biologist is more likely to think in evolutionary terms. Is there some advantage in such context-dependence?

As we have seen, Alex Kacelnic has distinguished among philosophical/psychological rationality (P-rationality), economic rationality (E-rationality), and biological rationality (B-rationality). To quote Kacelnic,

> B-rationality is necessarily linked to fitness maximization because it is based on the historical process of evolution. Evolutionary change is caused by both directional (natural selection) and non-directional (genetic drift). Both have some predictability. For instance, random genetic drift results in a predictable rate of accumulation of mutations and this serves as a clock to measure evolutionary distances between species. However, only natural selection generates phenotypic properties that can be anticipated using principles of maximization of a defined currency. For this reason,

biological rationality is best examined with natural selection (and hence fitness) at the centre.[51]

But is this really a question of rationality? If we think of animals as being rational in this sense, then by the same logic we should think of plants as being rational.

However, as Kalencher and Winterden[52] point out, animal models are an indispensible complement to the literature on human economic decision-making. Their perspective review starts from a description of the similarities in economic and evolutionary theories of human and animal decision-making, with particular emphasis on the optimality aspect that both classes of theories have in common. They note that empirically observed decisions often do not conform to the normative ideals of economic and ecological models, and that many of the behavioural violations found in humans can also be found in animals. They make the case that the sense or nonsense of the behavioural violations of optimality principles in humans can best be understood from an evolutionary perspective, thus requiring animal research.

Biologists think about optimal evolutionary strategies of both plants and animals, but the idea of B-rationality implies something about mechanism. It raises the question of what decision-making mechanisms are deployed by various animals. But this is a question about the biological bases of decision-making in general, which is the subject of the next chapter.

Points to remember

- Utility is a notional measure of the "value" of goods. It is a notional measure, because we do not know how it influences choice behaviour. But we can assume that utility (by definition) is maximized by a rational decision-maker.
- The basic economic principles apply not only to humans, but to many animal species, because animals have to allocate scarce means towards competing ends.
- Numerous studies of animals have shown that their demand functions follow the same general pattern as those of humans.
- If the decision-maker does not know for certain what the outcome will be, then the choice is either risky or uncertain. If some

probability can be associated with the consequences, then the choice of that activity is risky. If no probability can be associated with the consequences, the choice is simply uncertain.

- Risk sensitivity is common to humans and many other animal species. From an evolutionary viewpoint sensitivity to risk makes sense, but little is known about the mechanisms involved, so to assume that human risk sensitivity is a purely cognitive matter is questionable.

Further reading

Hurley, S. and Nudds, M. (eds) (2006) *Rational Animals*. Oxford University Press, Oxford.

Kalencher, T. and Winterden, M. (2011) Why we should use animals to study economic decision making: a perspective. *Front. Neurosci.*, 5, 82.

Sibly, R.M. and McCleery, R.H. (1983) Optimal decision rules for gulls. *Anim. Behav.*, 33, 449–465.

Tversky, A. and Kahneman, D. (1974) Judgement under uncertainty, heuristics and biases. *Sceince*, 185, 4157, 1124–1131.

Essential reading

Gowdy, John M. (2010) *Microeconomic Theory Old and New: A Students Guide*. Stanford University Press, Stanford, CA.

4
The Biological Bases of Decision-Making

Decisions

In this chapter we look at the biological bases of decision-making in general. We start by summarizing economic decision-making as discussed in the previous chapters, and then we proceed to discuss some biological, psychological, and philosophical aspects of decision-making in a wider context.

Recapitulation

There are two basic principles of standard economic decision-making. The first is that it must be rational, and the second is that it must involve some evaluation of the pros and cons of the situation. The basis of rational decision-making is that it should be self-consistent, a property that usually involves **transitivity of choice**. Suppose a person has to choose between options A, B, and C. If A is preferred to B, and B to C, then it is rational to expect that A will be preferred to C. We can now write a consistent order of preference, $A > B > C$. These relationships among A, B, and C are said to be transitive. If $A > B$ and $B > C$, but A is not preferred to C, then the decision to choose C above A is irrational, and the relationships among A, B, and C are intransitive. Economists base their theory upon the concept of the rational economic person, and this implies that all preference relationships are transitive. Rationality does not necessarily imply the use of reason. People may make some decisions as a result of reasoning, but they may also make rational decisions in a purely automatic way, as if designed or programmed to do so. People also sometimes make irrational decisions.

72

Economists have taken transitivity of choice as a working hypothesis, an assumption upon which the elementary theory is based. Transitivity of choice implies that something is maximized in the decision-making process. To see that this must be so, let us consider the following situation. Suppose A, B, and C can be evaluated numerically in some way. If A has a higher score than B, then we write A > B. A will be chosen over B by a person using a maximization principle (like choose the option with the larger score). If we know that B is larger than C, we can write B > C. If C is chosen over A, it would appear that C has been allocated a higher score than A, but we know that A > B > C, which implies that C has a lower score than A. Thus, if C is chosen over A, C must be preferred even though it has a lower score than A. A person making choices on this intransitive basis could not be choosing the option with the largest number of points; such a person could not be using a maximization principle. If a person's preferences are transitive, however, then we can deduce that he or she is using a maximizing principle, although the person may not be aware of it.

The name given to the quantity that is maximized in the choice behaviour of the rational economic person is utility. This is a *notional* measure of the psychological value of goods, leisure, and so on. It is called a notional measure because we do not know how it comes into people's choice behaviour. We only observe that they behave as if utility is maximized. Although, as we shall see, in reality, human choice behaviour is not always rational in the sense described above.

There is good experimental evidence that young children and monkeys do make transitive choices in behavioural tests, but this ability does not necessarily involve reasoning.[1] As we have seen, choice transitivity has been demonstrated in a number of species, but this should not imply that the mechanism is the same across all species.[2] Most economic decision theory is **normative** or prescriptive in that it is concerned with identifying the best decision to take. Biologists, on the other hand, are more interested in descriptive decisions. In other words, they want to know how animals make decisions, in the real world.

The biological view

Animals that make good decisions are likely to have greater fitness, but in terms of the life-history strategy that is typical of the species, a cheap and simple decision-making mechanism may be the best bet. For example, the lugworm *Arenicola* produces thousands of offspring (planctonic larvae). The worm lives in a U-shaped burrow in the littoral zone of muddy seashores and sand flats. The worm feeds from sand that is sucked into the head end of the burrow and this passes through the gut to be deposited on the surface at the tail end.

Feeding behaviour occurs in bursts that begin at regular seven-minute intervals and are separated by rest periods. The oxygen supply to the burrow is replenished by special irrigation behaviour that occurs regularly every fourth minute. The irrigation behaviour occurs, though less vigorously, even at low tide when oxygenated water is not available. The behaviour of *Arenicola* is dominated by rhythms that persist over a wide range of conditions. After a prolonged period of oxygen deprivation, however, the animal may break its rhythm and irrigate for a longer period that usual. Thus it appears that the behaviour of the animal is driven by a clock-like mechanism that is modified only in extreme circumstances. Such a rigid, programmed decision strategy may be suitable for an animal living in a stable and predictable environment, but a more flexible approach is required in more changeable situations.

Decision-making by the lugworm is very similar to that of a car-washing machine. The changes in behaviour are largely pre-programmed, backed up by seldom used emergency routines. A further step in sophistication can be added by endowing the animal, or machine, with the ability to change its state in response to changes in the outside world. In other words, what the animal sees, hears, or senses in any way, alters its internal state. Such an animal, or machine, behaves one way when in one state, and in another way when in another state. A person driving a car with a manual gearshift makes decisions as to when to change gear, but a person driving a car with an automatic gearshift makes no such decisions. The behaviour of the person-car entity could be the same in both cases. It makes no difference when talking about the person-car system whether the decisions to shift are made by the driver or by an automatic device. What matters is the way in which the **decision variables** (speed, engine revs per minute, etc.) are deployed. A decision of a person, animal, or robot is simply the process by which changes in the decision variables result in changes in behaviour. This biological viewpoint is very different from that normally found in the economics literature.

In the study of animal behaviour, decision-making is regarded as the process of changing from one activity to another, where there is incompatibility between the two activities. This terminology carries no implications about the mechanisms employed, whether reflex or deliberative. A distinction between design and execution is important in such studies. Generally, the design is seen as carried out by natural selection during the process of evolution, while the execution is the business of the individual animal. The design specifies what the animal "ought" to do in a given situation, and we should remember that the various possible activities differ in their consequences and have different costs and benefits attached to them. It is assumed that the animal is designed by natural selection to behave in such a manner that the greatest net benefit is attained. Thus there is a distinction between the ways *functional* and *causal* aspects of decision-making are understood; the former is often explained through optimality theory, the latter through experiments and some kind of causal modelling.

Functional aspects of decision-making

In biology the term function (of a trait) usually refers to the increase in reproductive success that the trait confers on its possessor's fitness, as we saw in Chapter 1. Functions are always complex and usually multiple. For example, the function of incubation in herring gulls is dependent upon a number of consequences of incubation: incubation keeps the eggs warm, but it prevents the sitter from foraging for food; it protects the eggs from predation, but it exposes the adult to attack by larger predators. Thus incubation has both costs and benefits. The function of incubation, therefore, has to be seen in terms of all the consequences of incubation that affect reproductive success, in comparison with the consequences of not incubating, or of incubating in a different manner.

These kinds of consideration have led biologists to apply optimality theory to the functional aspects of decision-making in animals. The best, or optimal, behaviour that an individual can perform in the given circumstances, in accordance with particular optimality criteria, can sometimes be recorded and calculated. For example, crows (*Corvus*) hunting for whelks at low tide usually select the largest ones. They then hover over a rock and drop the whelk so that it breaks open, exposing the edible inside. The number of times a whelk has to be dropped in order to break is related to the height of the drop. The crows have to expend energy in flying up to drop a whelk, so what is the best height for the crow to fly at? In other words, what is the optimal behaviour: to make many low flights, dropping the whelk each time, or to make few, higher flights? Given that the aim of the exercise (the optimality criterion) is to break open the whelk while expending the least amount of energy, it turns out that the optimal behaviour is for the crow to drop the whelk from a height of 5 metres, in which case it may have to make about five attempts, performing a total amount of upward flying of about 25 metres. For heights smaller or greater than 5 metres, a larger amount of total upward flying is required.[3]

In animal behaviour studies, optimality criteria are usually framed in terms of fitness. The ideal criterion would be inclusive fitness but this is normally impractical. In most studies, some short-term index of fitness is employed as the optimality criterion. For example, in studies of foraging behaviour, the notion of energy **profitability** is often the criterion used to judge the best foraging strategy. In other types of study, the concept of utility is the optimality criterion. Optimality criteria are important wherever there is a trade-off among the various costs and benefits of an activity. For example, a certain type of prey may be the most profitable for a foraging animal, but the time spent hunting that prey may also be time that the forager itself is exposed to predation. There is a trade-off between profitability and exposure time, in this case, and the optimality criteria must take into account both the energetic and the temporal aspects of foraging. Optimality criteria may be employed to calculate the optimal behaviour strategy or optimal design (e.g. of a limb), but the optimal solution is not always a stable one. For example, there are advantages and disadvantages of living in groups, and it would seem to follow that there should be an optimal group size for a particular species. However, if there were a group of the optimal size, then it would pay a solitary individual to join the group, thus pushing the group above the optimal size. The optimal group is unstable, and a stable group will, in practice, tend to be larger than the optimum.[4]

Note that an **evolutionary stable strategy**, in particular, cannot be an optimal strategy because, by definition, it cannot be bettered by any feasible alternative strategy, provided sufficient members of the population adopt it. Such **evolutionarily stable strategies** are found in cases where the best strategy for an individual depends upon the strategies adopted by other members of the population.

Trade-off

It is an inevitable consequence of the optimality approach to animal behaviour that there will be trade-offs among alternative courses of action. The logic of this conclusion is fairly simple. If the conditions relevant to only one activity pertain at a certain time (e.g. an animal in a Skinner box), then the optimal policy is straightforward. The animal engages in that activity and optimizes its pattern of behaviour with respect to the use of energy, time, and so on. If the conditions relevant to more than one activity pertain, then the animal has to choose between them, because the activities are incompatible (by definition[5]). In reality, animals often interleave the alternative activities, a phenomenon called **time-sharing**. For example, pigeons placed in a position where they can work for food or for water, do not complete one task before starting the other. They interleave the two in a manner that can be accounted for in terms of optimality theory.[6] Foraging sticklebacks change their pattern of predation when there is danger from predators. They achieve the optimal trade-off between attention to prey and predators.[7] Similarly, great tits change their pattern of foraging when their territory is threatened by rivals. They increase their vigilance at the expense of their food intake.[8]

So what about the human animal? The experimental physiologist Michel Cabanac, after studying trade-offs between aspects of physiology and behaviour in a variety of animals, turned his attention to humans. In one study he and his colleagues asked young male volunteers to report to the laboratory once per week to walk on a treadmill housed in a climatically controlled chamber.[9] In some sessions the slope of the treadmill was set by the experimenter at a specific gradient, and the subjects were asked to climb 300 metres. The speed of the treadmill was under the control of the subject. In other sessions, the speed of the treadmill was set by the experimenter and the slope of the treadmill under the control of the subject. The duration of all sessions was the time taken to climb 300 metres. The stride rate and heart rate of the subject was monitored.

The results showed that, after an adjustment period of about seven minutes, each subject made a rather constant choice of speed against slope, through altering whichever was under his control at the time.

The outcome was that the subjects adjusted speed and slope recip-rocally, with the result that the duration of sessions was constant. In other words, the subjects adjusted treadmill speed and slope to pro-duce an approximately constant ascending speed and physical power. In a similar set of experiments Cabanac found that subjects asked to trade-off treadmill slope and ambient temperature adjusted their behaviour to maintain their normal deep body temperature, and to limit their heart rate below 120 beats per minute.[10]

It is well established that a person's preferred walking gait is that with the highest mechanical efficiency and least oxygen cost. Like animals, people are capable of optimizing their behaviour to suit their physiological circumstances. In other words, they automatically trade-off those aspects of their behaviour and physiology that they control to achieve the best outcome. Note that the subjects in this type of experiment are not "conscious" of what they are doing. Their physiological trade-offs are subliminal.

In another set of experiments[11] 10 young males were invited to have lunch in the laboratory at their own usual time for lunch, and receive $12. Each came on four days, one preliminary session, and three experimental sessions. In the first session they were asked to eat one small (one mouthful) sandwich from each of 10 plates, and to give a magnitude-estimation verbal rating of the pleasantness (pos-itive rating) or unpleasantness (negative rating) of each item. The rating was to be a number of their own choice. After first eating 10 different sandwiches, the subject ate another one from each plate to modify (if necessary), the rating they had given to each type of sandwich. The subject was then told that he could eat whatever sandwiches were left, because he had been promised a meal. The total number of sandwiches eaten in this preliminary session by each subject was recorded.

In the experimental sessions, the price of each type of sandwich was set according to each subject's rating in the preliminary session. The subjects had to pay for sandwiches that they had rated positive, and were paid for sandwiches that they had rated negative. The rates of pay varied from one session to another, there being little differ-ence between the sandwich types in the first experimental session, medium differences in the second session, and large differences in the third session. Subjects were told to eat the same number of sand-wiches that they had eaten in the preliminary session. The subjects paid for their food out of the $12 that they were given for attending each session.

The results showed that not all subjects preferred the same sandwiches. However, the price rank-order of the 10 types of sandwich presented to each subject was based upon their preferences as revealed in the preliminary session. The results of the first experimental session showed that the subjects ate mostly medium and high palatability sandwiches, but no low palatability sandwiches, although they could have received a small amount of money for eating the latter. In the second experimental session, the subjects ate sandwiches from all the plates. In the third session they ate sandwiches from all the plates, but the majority were taken from the low palatability plates.

These results are entirely consistent with the mathematical predictions made on the basis of the pricing of the sandwiches in the three experimental sessions. The hypothesis underlying these predictions was that the subjects should eat more sandwiches whose palatability outweighed the price than sandwiches that were not worth the price. Cleverly, the relative weighting given the palatability and price indices was different in the three experimental sessions.[12] In other words, the subjects could trade-off palatability versus money in the same way that they could trade-off purely physiological variables in other experiments. In similar experiments, Cabanac has shown that people can trade-off money versus pain and money versus cold discomfort.[13] Note that subjects in this type of experiment, if asked, find it difficult to be explicit (i.e. give reasons) about their behaviour. The same goes for the experiments mentioned in Chapter 1, where subjects put up with pain to allow their relatives to receive small amounts of money.

In another experiment, Cabanac pitted thermal discomfort against the pleasure of playing a video game.[14] In the first part of the experiment the subject played the video game for one hour, and every five minutes was requested to rate, on a magnitude-estimation scale, the pleasure of playing the video game. In the second session the subject (without playing the video game) was subjected to a progressively declining temperature (from 25 to 7 degrees centigrade) for over one hour, and every five minutes was requested to rate the pleasure/displeasure aroused by the ambient temperature. "No anchor (landmark) was given for the ratings; the only instruction received by the subjects was to use positive figures for pleasure and negative figures for displeasure."[15] In the third session, both video game and falling ambient temperature were presented simultaneously, and the only instruction received by the subjects was that they could terminate the session whenever they wanted to. The pertinent result of the experiment was how long the subject remained in this situation. The hypothesis under test was that at each instant the subject will tend to maximize the algebraic sum of his ratings. It could therefore be expected that the subject would end the session when the sum of the ratings in the first two sessions reached zero. Cabanac was thus able to compare the theoretical and actual durations endured by each subject. His predictions were spot on; he was able to predict with remarkable accuracy the subjects' trade-offs between the positive effect of playing the video game and the negative effects of the ambient temperature.

The trade-off principle is simply a statement that, if all alternatives are properly traded-off within a system, then that process maximizes some entity. Whether this entity is necessarily a scalar quantity is debatable. In Cabanac's case, he insists on calling the maximized entity "pleasure", but it does not really matter what the entity is called. Cabanac's experiments, and other work on animal trade-offs taken together with the work on animal economics,[16] strongly suggest that animals have an internal coherence (of their behaviour and physiology), and that this is also true of humans. In fact, the finding that people behave as they do in very animal-like situations (e.g. the treadmill experiment) supports the view that animals and humans operate in the same way.

The evidence shows that the trade-off principle operates across many species.[17] This suggests that the fundamentals of decision-making are the same in those species. When it comes to humans, there is an issue as to whether the maximized quantity is implicit (e.g. utility), or explicit (e.g. pleasure). For biologists, there are questions regarding whether the trade-offs are simply embedded in the machinery, or whether they are able to be altered by learning and/or cognition. Biologists also have difficulties with undue anthropomorphism, the tendency to attribute human qualities to animals. The problem is that it is part of human nature to do so, an "incurable disease".[18] Some biologists maintain that they cannot make themselves understood without resorting to such language.[19] In other words, subjects in such trade-off experiments find it difficult to give "reasons" for their behaviour, and experimenters on animals in trade-off situations find it difficult to explain what is going on without resorting to anthropomorphic language.

"Voluntary" decisions

We normally think of human economic decisions as being voluntary, but what does that actually mean? The legal view stems largely from the philosophical notion of **action**, behaviour caused by a mental state, such as an *intent*. Thus action results from the nexus of *belief, desire*, and *intent*, all of which are mental states. Moreover, a *rational person* is expected to be able to give a *reason* for their action. As we shall see, philosophers vary considerably in their attitude to action.

In physiological terms, voluntary movement in vertebrates is conducted by the somatic nervous system, while the autonomic nervous system controls involuntary activities, such as vomiting, and so on. The somatic system controls the skeletal muscles, so that, in everyday terms, if we wish to move in a certain way, we can do so as an act of "will". However, there are a number of somatic reflexes, such as righting oneself after stumbling, that are automatic. Moreover, there is a "fuzzy area" in which changes in behaviour are subliminal. For example, I may desire and intend to have a sleep, but the act of falling asleep is subliminal. So whether I can rightly say that I decided to fall asleep is questionable. Similarly in economic decision-making there is a possibility, which we shall explore, that some such decisions are subliminal.

Introspection

Some psychologists have argued that introspection is not a good guide to our cognitive reality. "Introspection does not provide a direct pipeline to nonconscious mental processes. Instead, it is best thought of as a process whereby people use the contents of consciousness to construct a personal narrative that may or may not correspond to their nonconscious states."[20] This view stems from the pioneering work of Nisbett and Wilson (1977) who reported on experiments in which subjects verbally explained why they had a particular preference, or how they arrived at a particular idea. On the basis of these studies they concluded that reports on mental processes are confabulated, in that the subjects had little or no introspective access to higher order cognitive processes.

The term "introspection illusion" is attributed to Emily Pronin.[21] The illusion has been examined in psychological experiments, and has been suggested as a basis for biases when people compare themselves to others. These experiments have been interpreted as suggesting that introspection is a process of construction and inference, rather than offering direct access to the processes underlying the mental states. Pronin describes the illusion as having four components:

- People give a strong weighting to introspective evidence when assessing themselves.
- People do not give introspective evidence strong weight when assessing others.
- People tend to disregard their own behaviour when assessing themselves, but they do not disregard the behaviour of others.
- It is not simply that people lack access to each other's introspections – they only regard their own as reliable.

It would appear that introspection does not provide a direct pipeline to non-conscious mental processes. Instead it is best thought of as a process whereby people use the contents of consciousness to construct a personal narrative that may or may not correspond to their non-conscious states. This is the view taken by Timothy Wilson and Elizabeth Dunn[22] in their review of the research in this field.

If we go back to the Cabanac-type of experiment described in Chapter 1, in which subjects put up with pain in order to have a small amount of money sent to a relative[23] it is indeed difficult to imagine what is going through their mind. They may feel that they have a certain obligation to the experimenter, having volunteered in the first place. Nevertheless, they still "calibrate" their effort according to their degree of relatedness to the intended recipient of a very small amount of money. It looks as though, whatever "reasons" a person may give for their behaviour, they will not be believed by the type of psychologist involved in introspection research. This brings us to a more philosophical argument.

The teleological imperative

Mental entities have a property that western philosophers call **intentionality**.[24] In its current usage, intentionality refers to that property of the mind by which it is directed at, or about, or of, objects and states of affairs in the world. Human intentionality includes such mental phenomena as belief, desire, intention, hope, fear, love, hate, lust, and disgust.

An action, in philosophical terminology, is something that a person does voluntarily, as opposed to something like snoring, which is involuntary. People are taken to be morally responsible for their actions if they are the cause of the action and could have done otherwise. A person doing something intentionally (or on purpose) results from that person *desiring* something and *believing* something, and therefore having a *reason* for doing something (the action). Thus action results from the nexus of *desire, belief,* and *intent.* Moreover, a *rational person* is expected to be able to give a *reason* for their action. A *reason* is a kind of explanation in terms of *desire* and *belief.* For example, the *reason* that I bought this bird is that I *desired* a singing bird, and I *believed* that this bird was a canary, and that a canary is a kind of singing bird.

Needless to say, philosophers vary considerably in their attitude to action. Some hold that all actions are performed as a result of a person having a reason (i.e. they hold that reasons can be causes). Others maintain that actions are movements that we are aware of making, but still others claim that (for example) picking up a glass and drinking water whilst engrossed in conversation is an action of which we are not aware. Most philosophers insist that actions are aspects of behaviour that involve an **explicit representation** of a goal-to-be achieved (in other words a **goal-directed** action). By goal-directed action they mean behaviour that is mediated by **explicit knowledge** of the causal relationship between the action and its outcome. For example, I enter a room to find my book, but I can't see in the dark. If I operate this switch, then the light will come on. My goal is to be able to see well enough to find my book. I know that (explicit knowledge) switching on the light is an action that will enable me to find my book. However, it is possible to account for this series of events without recourse to the concept of goal-directed action.[25]

A goal-directed system involves a representation of the goal-to-be-achieved, which is instrumental in guiding the behaviour. The term goal-directed applies to that behaviour (of a human, animal, or machine) directed by reference to an internal (implicit or explicit) representation of the goal-to-be-achieved. By directed we mean that the behaviour is actively controlled by reference to the (internally represented) goal. The behaviour may be subject to outside disturbance that will usually be corrected for. Thus by directed we mean that the behaviour is guided or steered towards the goal, despite disturbances.

An everyday way of saying the same thing is to say that the behaviour is *intentional*. However, this term is not usually used in describing the goal-directed behaviour of animals or robots, because these are assumed to be devoid of that property that philosophers call intentionality, that property of the mind by which it is directed at, or about, objects and states of affairs in the world. For an animal or robot to have intentionality, it would have to have a mind. There may be some who embrace such an idea, but most western philosophers would assume that intentionality is a property restricted to the human mind.

Goal-directed behaviour is not the only way of arriving at a goal. A **goal-achieving** system is a system that can "recognize" the goal once it is arrived at, but the process of arriving at the goal is largely a matter of circumstance, or the result of built-in trade-off mechanisms. Consider a collector of old matchboxes. The collector does not set out to search for rare matchboxes, but relies upon serendipity – the phenomenon of making sudden and unexpected discoveries by accident. The goal is achieved by being in the right place at the right time and recognizing a desirable matchbox for what it is. Now consider a person walking a long distance. As we have seen, it is well established that a person's preferred walking pace is that which combines the highest mechanical efficiency (which depends upon the length of their legs) with the least oxygen cost. This is achieved by internal physiological trade-offs of which the person is not aware.

Goal-seeking behaviour seeks a goal without the goal being represented within the system. An example is the habitat selection of the common woodlouse (*Porcellio scaber*). These animals move about in an irregular manner, but their movements are more rapid in dry than in moist air. The result is that the animals spend more time in damp places, thus achieving a simple form of habitat selection.

We would not normally think of goal-seeking, or goal-achieving, behaviour as being intentional. We might say that nature intends the woodlouse to be goal-achieving, but this is just short-hand for a functional (i.e. evolutionary) argument. In our ordinary folk psychology, we would regard only goal-directed behaviour to be intentional. However, this kind of stance is basically **teleological**[26] in the sense that a representation of the goal dictates or controls the behaviour that is to reach the goal. So in ordinary language, if I say that I intend to write an essay, then others will expect me to set about writing an essay. However it might be more truthful to say "I have in mind writing an essay". If I say I intend to write an essay, I do not mean that I will write an essay, no matter what, because events may intervene, or I may change my mind.

Goal-directed behaviour is designed to achieve the goal no matter what, because the (negative-feedback) design is such that alternative activities are suppressed. Such a design is incompatible with the trade-off-principle, because active (goal-directed) control systems are designed to eliminate the influence of extraneous variables, whereas the essential feature of trade-off is to allow such influences.[27] This may be so in animals, but some are convinced that human brains are (uniquely) able to combine flexibility in setting up new goals, coupled with tenacity and inflexibility in pursuing them.[28] Be that as it may, there are two points to be made here. Firstly, humans may maintain the trade-off principles inherited from their animal ancestors (and demonstrated by Cabanac's experiments), and at the same time (with some incompatibility) be capable of genuine intentions. In other words, the two postulated mechanisms are compromised by each other. Secondly, "Introspection tells us that much of our own behaviour is intentional, and we tend to assume that the behaviour of other people, of some animals, and even of some machines, is similar."[29] In other words, "We are designed to think in teleological terms. This mode of thinking is useful in interpreting the behaviour of our political rivals."[30] The suggestion is that, "Our evolutionary inheritance pre-disposes us to interpret the world in terms of meanings and purposes, as if the rivalries of our political life were relevant to the inanimate world. The result is that we attribute purpose where there is no purpose, and seek meaning where there is no meaning."[31]

It would not be surprising if a highly social primate species, in the process of developing language, would find it necessary to distinguish between "deliberate" and "accidental" behaviour. Such a distinction would enable blame to be levied where appropriate. Consequently, "We (now) talk and think in teleological terms...we find it very hard to divorce ourselves from the purposive anthropomorphic view, which I propose to call the teleological imperative".[32]

Robert Trivers has suggested that deception is a fundamental aspect of communication in nature. It is employed by both plants and animals. Examples include **mimicry**, **injury-feigning**,[33] and **deceit**. Those who are better able to perceive deception are more likely to survive. As a result, self-deception evolved to better mask deception from those who perceive it well, as Trivers puts it: "Hiding the truth from yourself to hide it more deeply from others."[34]

There is a strong pressure of natural selection to recognize when deception occurs. As a result, self-deception has evolved so as to better hide the signs of deception from others. The proposal is that an innate ability to commit self-deception enables the deceiver to hide the deceit. Humans deceive themselves in order to better deceive others and thus have an advantage over them. In the three decades since Trivers introduced his adaptive theory of self-deception, there has been an ongoing debate over the question of whether such behaviour has a genetic basis. An example of human self-deception is the common occurrence of the alcoholic who is self-deceived in believing that his drinking is under control.

There is a certain similarity between the teleological imperative view and the self-deception view. In both cases there is an implied evolutionary advantage in misleading other members of the same species in order to gain what is essentially a "political" advantage.

Whither *Homo economicus*?

One of the "take home" messages of this book is that many animal species, including humans, have innate, sophisticated physiological and behavioural trade-off mechanisms that enable them to "do the right thing". The evidence for this comes primarily from experiments, but also from applications of optimality theory.

One result of these trade-off abilities is that the animals concerned exhibit the "classical" microeconomic phenomena. It would, therefore, seem somewhat unaccommodating to claim that humans have a superior way of dealing with such economic situations. On the other hand, humans clearly to have some "mental" abilities that other animals lack. Some have suggested that there is something unnatural about *Homo economicus*. For example, whereas *Homo economicus* maximizes utility in terms of self-interest, the anthropological evidence[35] shows that humans in a more natural state (i.e. hunter-gatherers) are much more reciprocal in their outlook (sometimes dubbed *Homo reciprocans*).[36] Secondly, in the real world (as opposed to the laboratory) deals are reached that are, in effect, compromises. For example, a shopkeeper who has set a price for a product is often willing to settle for a lower price, if they particularly need a sale at that time. A customer who wants the product, but is not willing to pay the price, may suggest a lower price and secure the shopkeeper's agreement. But if the customer suggests a price that is too low, the shopkeeper is likely to take offence, and refuse. So there is a mix here of the value of the product to the customer, the initial hopes of the shopkeeper, and the pride of the shopkeeper (who is mindful of their reputation within the community).

Reciprocal players are willing to reward behaviour that is just or fair, and to punish unjust or unfair behaviour. Empirical evidence suggests that positive and negative reciprocity are fundamentally different behavioural dispositions in the sense that the values for positive and negative reciprocity in individuals are only weakly correlated and that these values correlate differently with factors such as gender or age.[37] A possible explanation is that negative and positive reciprocity are different because they tap into different emotional responses.[38] The degree of reciprocity in the natural environment is likely to be related to kinship, and to future social prospects with neighbouring tribes. Recent sociological studies show that positive reciprocity correlates with health indicators such as height, with increasing age, with female gender, and with higher income. In addition, higher number of hours of work, a higher number of friends, and higher over-all life satisfaction correlate positively with reciprocity.[39]

It may well be that people with a comfortable lifestyle, such as hunter-gatherers and relatively well-off money-earners, are more inclined towards reciprocity than people near the bread-line. On the other hand, within poor communities there is often a lot of sharing of child-care, food, and other goods.

So who is *Homo economicus*? Does he exist? Did he ever exist? Historically, he certainly existed in the minds of certain economists. But did they live in the real world? Certainly much current economic research does not take place in the real world, as we saw in Chapter 3. Indeed, the evidence suggests that both humans and other animals obey the classic economic laws when tested in the laboratory, but deviate from these laws in the real world.

How is it that many other species behave like *Homo economicus* under certain conditions? It may be that humans have inherited a certain economic savvy from their remote ancestors. This would account for the similarities between *Homo economicus* and other species. But then modern humans have a much greater cognitive capacity than other primates, and possibly all other animal species. So maybe the human "natural" economic responses sit uncomfortably with their other recently evolved mental capacities. Possibly, the human ability for complex trade-offs (that they share with other species) is not fully "joined up" with their language and consequent mental abilities.

Points to remember

- Choice transitivity has been demonstrated in a number of species, but the mechanism may not be the same across all species.
- A decision of a person, animal, or robot is simply the process by which changes in the decision variables result in changes in behaviour. This biological viewpoint is very different from that normally found in the economics literature.
- In biology, the term function (of a trait) usually refers to the increase in reproductive success that the trait confers on its possessor's *fitness*. Functions are always complex and usually multiple.
- It is an inevitable consequence of the optimality approach to animal behaviour that there will be trade-offs among alternative courses of action. The evidence shows that the trade-off principle operates across many species. This suggests that the fundamentals of decision-making are the same in those species.
- When it comes to humans, there is an issue as to whether the maximized quantity is implicit (e.g. utility), or explicit (e.g. pleasure).
- Some psychologists have argued that introspection is not a good guide to our cognitive reality. Some biologists have suggested that self-deceit, and the teleological imperative have evolved in humans to serve social, or political, functions.

Further reading

Kennedy, J. (1992) *The New Anthropomorphism.* Cambridge University Press, Cambridge.

McFarland, D., Stenning, K. and McGonigle-Chalmers, M. (eds) (2012) *The Complex Mind. An Interdisciplinary Approach.* Palgrave Macmillan, Houndmills, Basingstoke.

Montefiore, A. and Noble, D. (eds) (1989) *Goals, No Goals and Own Goals.* Unwin Hyman, London.

Essential reading

Kahneman, D. (2011) *Thinking, Fast and Slow.* Allen Lane, Penguin.

Glossary

Action A form of *goal-directed* behaviour, having the appearance of being intentional. Normally applied only to humans. There are many philosophical theories of action, and it is not possible to give a single, generally agreed upon, definition of an action. Probably, the most widely held view amongst philosophers is the causal theory, which maintains that the difference between a movement pattern and an action is that the latter is accompanied by a particular kind of mental event, which plays a causal role, whereas the former is not so accompanied. Basically, action theories are *goal-directed* theories, because they envisage a mental state of affairs that is related to the goal (i.e. some form of knowing about the likely consequences) that is instrumental in guiding the behaviour.

Altruism Self-destructive behaviour performed for the benefit of others. This biological usage contains no implications about intentions or motives. An important question is what is meant by benefit. One possibility is to regard the cost to the altruist and the benefit to the recipient as being measured in units of *inclusive fitness*. This is defined in such a way that natural selection would not be expected to favour animals that improved the inclusive fitness of others at the expense of their own. Parental care would not qualify as altruism by this definition, for by caring for its young an animal increases its own fitness. Another possibility is to define cost and benefit in terms of simple survival chances. An altruistic act then becomes one that decreases the altruist's chances of surviving, while increasing the survival chances of some other individual, the beneficiary. Parental care increases the survival chances of the offspring, while it decreases the life expectancy of the parent. In genetic terms, genes for parental care tend to be preserved in the bodies of the surviving offspring, and such genes are, therefore, likely to increase in frequency relative to the genes that promote neglect towards offspring. Thus altruism at the individual level is a manifestation of "selfishness" at the gene level.

Autoshaping A type of learning in which the animal develops a response without special training. Take, for example, pigeons in a Skinner box pecking at a key. Usually, the key is illuminated and the light is extinguished when the key is pecked. If pigeons are presented with repeated pairings of key illumination and food reward, they begin to peck the key without any prior training. This *autoshaping* phenomenon is the result of a straightforward *classical conditioning* situation. The lighted key is paired with grain, and the pigeon comes to peck the key as if it were grain. The point can be demonstrated even more clearly if key illumination is paired with a reward to which pecking is not the pigeon's natural response. This can be done by offering a sexual reward. Paired male and female pigeons are housed in adjacent chambers, separated

90

by a sliding door. Once a day the stimulus light is turned on and the sliding door is removed, so that the male can begin his courtship display for a minute or so. Within five to 10 trials the male pigeon begins to make conditioned sexual responses towards the stimulus light. The pigeons direct their courtship towards the light, thus behaving as if it were a female.

Classical conditioning The type of learning first studied by Pavlov, in which the animal forms an association between a significant stimulus (the unconditional stimulus) and a neutral stimulus (the conditional stimulus). After repeated exposure to the paired stimuli, the animal's response to the unconditional stimulus (the unconditional response) can be elicited by the conditional stimulus alone. This response (the conditional response) is not always exactly the same as the unconditional response.

Co-adaptation Mutual adaptation: separate structures or facets of behaviour are designed by *natural selection* specifically for interaction with each other. Co-adaptation may occur among parts of a single organism. For example, certain light-coloured moths prefer to rest on light-coloured surfaces, and dark-coloured moths on dark surfaces. This coadaptation of coloration and behaviour functions to improve camouflage. Co-adaptation between organisms may be intraspecific or interspecific. The former refers to coadaptation between organisms of the same species. For example, in communicating it is important that a signal sent by one individual is coadapted to the receiving apparatus of another. Interspecific coadaptation refers to complementary adaptation between members of different species. Thus pollinating insects possess morphology and behaviour that is tailored specifically to the requirements of certain plants. Likewise, the plant structure is coadapted to specific pollinating insects.

Coefficient of genetic relatedness, r A measure of the probability that a gene in one individual will be identical by descent to a gene in a particular relative. An equivalent and alternative measure is the proportion on an individual's genome that is identical by descent to the relative's genome. Note that the genes must be identical by descent and not simply genes shared by the population as a whole. This means that r is the probability that a gene common to two individuals is descended from the same ancestral gene in a recent common relative.

Cost of changing The decrement in fitness that arises when an animal is changing from one activity to another, and receiving benefits from neither. The cost may involve loss of valuable time, expenditure of energy, or risk from predators.

Deceit A form of *evolutionary strategy* involving communication. Deceit occurs when the signaller's fitness increases at the expense of the receiver's. For example, many ground-nesting birds feign injury when their nest is approached by a predator, such as a fox. The bird moves away from the nest trailing an apparently broken wing, thus luring the fox away from the nest. This type of distraction display is not usually regarded as a deliberate ploy on the part of the individual animal, but rather an instinctive reaction to an approaching predator. A common form of deceit is mimicry in which one animal (the mimic) resembles another animal (the model), so that a predator is confused. Often the model is avoided by the predator, and this avoidance is extended to the mimic. For example, birds that avoid wasps also avoid the similar but harmless hoverflies, because they have similar warning colouration. For a deceitful strategy to be successful, it is important that the misleading signals occur rarely in relation to normal signals. Otherwise receivers will (via natural selection) adjust their rules for decoding signals.

Decision variables The variables upon which decisions are made, and in terms of which a common currency is based. For example, in deciding between chalk and cheese, the common currency might be weight.

Demand function A concept used in economics to express the relationship between the price and the consumption of a commodity. For example, when the price of coffee is increased and people continue to buy the same amount as before, demand is said to be inelastic. When the price of fish is increased, and people buy less than before, demand is said to be elastic. Exactly analogous phenomena occur in animal behaviour. If an animal expends a certain amount of energy on a particular activity, then it usually does less of that activity if the energy requirement is increased. The elasticity of demand functions in animals gives an indication of the relative importance of the various activities in the animal's repertoire. Demand functions are closely related to behavioural *resilience.*

Evolutionarily stable strategy An *evolutionary strategy* that cannot be bettered by any feasible alternative strategy, provided sufficient members of the population adopt it. Often, the best strategy for an individual depends upon the strategies adopted by other members of the population, and the resulting strategy may be a mixture of a number of strategies. For example, two participants in a contest may not have the same choice of strategies, or prospective payoffs. In contests between male and female, old and young, or the owner of a resource and a non-owner, an asymmetry may be perceived beforehand by the contestants, and will usually influence the choice of action. Such situations are usually analysed in terms of game theory.

Evolutionary discordance A discordance between the present situation and the situation to which the organism is evolutionarily adapted.

Evolutionary strategy A passive result of natural selection that gives the appearance of a ploy employed by genes to increase their numbers at the expense of other genes. An evolutionary strategy is not a strategy in the cognitive sense, but a theoretical tool employed by evolutionary biologists.

Exogamy A social arrangement where sexual intercourse is allowed outside of a social group. Social rules define its scope and extent. Exogamy has both biological and cultural aspects.

Explicit knowledge Knowledge depends upon representations. Implicit knowledge (sometimes called *procedural knowledge*), or know-how, is based upon *implicit representations*. This type of knowledge has to do with accomplishing skilled tasks, such as capturing prey. In everyday life we call this knowing how to do something, such as ride a bicycle. Explicit knowledge is knowledge that involves *explicit representations* of facts that are accessible to a number of processes, and not simply part of a fixed procedure. In human terms, explicit knowledge would imply knowledge of facts that could be put to many uses. Thus knowing that fire is hot can be useful in cooking food, clearing land, repelling predators, and so on. Whether animals have explicit knowledge is controversial.

Explicit representation A representation that can be put to many uses. The basis of explicit knowledge.

Fitness A biological and mathematical concept akin to survival value, which indicates the ability of genetic material to perpetuate itself in the course of evolution. The concept of fitness may be applied to single genes and to the genetic make-up (genotype) of individual animals, or to animal groups. In animal behaviour, the concept most widely employed is the fitness of a genotype relative to other genotypes in the population. An animal's *individual fitness* is a measure of the relative ability of the animal to leave viable offspring. All factors that affect the animal's fertility and fecundity will affect its individual fitness. These include the morphological, physiological, and behavioural characteristics of the animal. The process of *natural selection* determines which characteristics confer greater relative fitness, but the effectiveness of natural selection depends upon the mix of genotypes in the population. Thus, the relative fitness of a genotype depends upon the environmental conditions and the other genotypes present in the population. The *inclusive fitness* of an animal is a measure based upon the number of the animal's genes that are present in subsequent generations, rather than the number of offspring. In assessing the inclusive fitness of an animal, it is necessary to take account of the number of its genes that are also present in related individuals. This will depend upon the *coefficient of relationship* between one individual and another.

Goal The state of affairs that brings a particular activity to an end. This may be internal to the animal, such as consummatory behaviour (e.g. eating) that brings to an end a period of appetitive behaviour (e.g. seeking food). It is helpful to distinguish among goal-achieving, goal-seeking, and goal-directed behaviour. A *goal-achieving* system is one that can recognize the goal once it is arrived at, but the process of arriving at the goal is largely determined by environmental circumstances. A *goal-seeking* system is one that is designed to seek the goal without the goal being represented explicitly within the system. Many physical systems are of this type. A *goal-directed* system involves an explicit representation of the goal-to-be-achieved, which is instrumental in directing the behaviour. In animal behaviour it is sometimes postulated that the animal possesses a "search image". Such an animal would be capable of goal-directed behaviour. The various types of goal-oriented behaviour are important in accounting for the apparently purposive and *intentional* behaviour in humans.

Handling time The time taken to secure the food item. Animals must expend energy in order to forage, and there may be circumstances in which the energy available to spend is limited. Similarly, there may be a limited amount of time available for foraging, and the rate at which a forager can harvest prey may also be constrained. In particular, the **handling time** required to recognize, capture, and process each food item may place a limit on the harvesting rate.

Heuristic refers to experience-based techniques for problem-solving, decision-making, and so on. Mental short-cuts, or rules-of-thumb, are used to arrive at a solution that might otherwise be time consuming.

Hoarding The storage of food, or other things, either in a central cache, or distributed throughout a home range or territory. Storing food in a single, large cache, sometimes called *larder hoarding*, occurs in many small mammals, and in some birds and insects. Acorn woodpeckers, for example, live in small groups and prepare trees by drilling hundreds of evenly spaced holes in tree trunks and branches. Each hole is filled with an acorn. Bumblebees (*Bombus* and other genera) construct separate vessels in their nests for the storage of pollen and nectar. *Scatter hoarding*, the storage of food in many dispersed sites, is common in many birds and mammals. The grey squirrel stores food in holes that it digs in the ground, which are carefully covered with leaves and grass. Crows, jays, magpies, and nutcrackers do the same. Food hoarding serves many functions. Periods of low food availability can be survived by eating food stored during periods of abundance. Jays rear their young on stored food that would otherwise be unavailable when the young are in the nest. Carnivores, such as leopards and weasels, cache prey to prevent its loss to scavengers. Animals that do not hoard food often exploit food stored by others. Willow tits follow food-hoarding coal tits and rob their caches. Scatter hoarders and larder hoarders deal with this type of parasitism in different ways. Larder hoarders vigorously defend their caches. Scatter hoarders cannot do this, and instead they reduce the likelihood of losing their caches by spacing them out and using a variety of types of place for storage. Scatter hoarding makes it uneconomical for other animals to exploit the caches, but it also presents the hoarding animal with the problem of recovering its own stored food. Some species are known to remember accurately the location of their many caches. The red fox, the common jay, and the marsh tit all remember the location of hoarded food and readily find it again.

Imitation An aspect of cultural behaviour which involves the ability to copy aspects of the behaviour of another individual. Some phenomena, such as *social facilitation*, may give the appearance of imitation, but they do not involve true copying.

Imprinting An aspect of learning that takes place during a sensitive period in the early stages of an animal's life. For example, lambs follow the person that has reared them on a bottle. Even after the lamb has been weaned and joined the flock, it will approach its former keeper, and try to stay nearby. If the lamb has grown into a mature male, it may show a sexual interest in its keeper. The lamb is imprinted upon the keeper, and this has both short- and long-term aspects. The lamb follows the keeper when young, and as an adult it shows some attachment to its keeper.

Inclusive fitness A measure of *fitness* based upon the number of the animal's genes that are present in subsequent generations, rather than the number of offspring. In assessing the inclusive fitness of an animal it is necessary to take account of the number of its genes that are also present in related individuals. This will depend upon the *coefficient of relatedness* between the one individual and another.

Indifference curves Curves that connect points (on a graph) of equal value.

Injury-feigning A form of behaviour used by birds and fish to distract the attention of a predator and lure it away from a nest or vulnerable young. Typically, a ground-living bird, such as a plover, will feign an injury (e.g. a broken wing) and "limp" away from its nest.

Intentionality That property of the mind by which it is directed at, or about, objects and states of affairs in the world. It includes such mental phenomena as belief, desire, and intention.

Labour supply curve A curve joining points on a graph of wage rate against hours. It shows how a change in wage rate affects the number of hours (per day) that a worker is willing to work.

Life expectancy The average number of years that a human (or other animal) has before death, conventionally calculated from the time of birth. Note that this measure includes infant deaths.

Life-history strategy An *evolutionary strategy* relating to the expenditure of energy (on growth and reproduction) throughout the lifetime of the individual.

Limbo A state in which an animal has "time on its hands" as a result of having performed all normal time-consuming activities (e.g. feeding, sleeping). Such a situation would not arise in nature, because the animal would be "programmed" for activities such as migration, reproduction, and hibernation. In captivity where such activities are not possible the animal is said to be in limbo, a concept sometimes used in the study of animal boredom.

Mimicry The resemblance of one animal (the mimic) to another animal (the model) such that the two are confused. In *Batesian mimicry* the predator avoids a noxious animal producing a particular signal (the model), and is deceived into avoiding an edible mimic which produces a similar signal. It is of advantage to the mimic, but no advantage to the model. In *Müllerian mimicry* a group of noxious species share the same warning signals, such as the black and yellow patterns of wasps.

Motivation A reversible aspect of the animal's state that plays a causal role in behaviour (as opposed to irreversible changes due to injury, learning, and maturation). An animal's motivational state changes continually as a result of both external and internal changes.

Natural selection The process by which evolution of living organisms occurs. Evidence for evolution comes from the fossil record, comparison of present-day species, the geographical distribution of species, and some observations of evolution in action. Natural selection determines the survival value of a trait (such as body colour). That is, the extent to which a trait is passed from one generation to the next, in a wild population, is determined by the breeding success of the parental generation, and the value of the trait in enabling the individuals to survive natural hazards, such as food shortage, predators, and sexual rivals. Such environmental pressures can be looked upon as selecting those inheritable variations that best fit or adapt the animal to its environment.

Normative decisions (or prescriptive decisions) are those decisions that are the best in practice.

Optimal foraging theory Optimal behaviour is the best behaviour that an individual can perform in the given circumstances, in accordance with particular "optimality criteria" – the criteria in relation to which it is possible to determine which of a set of alternatives is the best. In animal behaviour studies, optimality criteria are preferably framed in terms of *fitness*, but this is not always practical. In most studies, some short-term index of fitness is employed as the optimality criterion. For example, in studies of foraging behaviour, the notion of *profitability* is often the criterion used to judge the best foraging strategy. In other types of study, the concept of *utility* is the optimality criterion. Optimality criteria are important wherever there is a *trade-off* among the various costs and benefits of an activity. For example, a certain type of prey may be the most profitable for a foraging animal, but the time spent hunting that prey may also be time that the forager itself is exposed to predation. There is a trade-off between profitability and exposure time in this case, and the optimality criteria must take into account both the energetic and the temporal aspects of foraging.

Procedural knowledge Knowledge relating to a procedure of skill. Also called knowledge how, or know-how.

Profitability The beneficial result of activities such as foraging (in terms of energy) or trading (in terms of money).

Rational decision-making Decision-making that maximizes a quantity (usually called *utility*). Such decision-making does not, necessarily, have anything to do with reasoning, or reason-giving.

Reciprocal altruism An aspect of *altruism* in which one animal helps another at some cost to itself in the "expectation" that it will be the recipient of altruism at a later date. The problem with the evolution of this kind of altruism is that individuals who cheat, by receiving but never giving, can be at an advantage.

Reproductive value An age-related indicator of reproductive success. The *fitness* of a genotype in a Darwinian sense can be measured in terms of the number of its progeny. The age-specific reproductive value is an index of the extent to which the members of a given age group contribute to the next generation, between now and when they die.

Resilience The extent to which an activity is resistant to pressures of time. Low-resilience activities are those that are curtailed when time is short, because other (high-resilience) activities take priority. An activity that is abandoned under these conditions may be regarded as a leisure activity.

Rule of thumb A rule based on practice or experience, rather than theory.

Sexual selection A form of *natural selection* which depends upon the advantage that certain individuals have over others of the same sex and species solely in respect of reproduction.

Social facilitation A form of apparent imitation that may occur as a result of a tendency to investigate places where other members of the species has been observed. Examples include a tendency to eat what others are eating, and to avoid food items shunned by others.

Spheres of exchange A heuristic tool, used by anthropologists, for analysing trading restrictions within societies that are communally governed and where resources are communally available. Typically, goods or services of specific types are relegated to distinct categories, and sanctions are invoked to prevent exchange between these categories. For example, if food items may be exchanged for food items, but not for tools, then food and tools are involved in different spheres of exchange.

Stereotypy Any behaviour that is repetitive and relatively fixed in form. Examples include habitual or routine behaviour, including behaviour that is necessarily repetitive, such as digging. *Stereoptypies* often appears under conditions of stress.

Teleological Relating to purpose or function.

Territory An area or patch of ground defended by an animal against members of the same species.

Time-sharing A situation in which a motivationally dominant activity makes time for a sub-dominant activity.

Tolerance The ability to tolerate extreme values of environmental factors, such as temperature, humidity, and so on.

Trade-off Balancing of priorities, either as an aspect of *function*, or of *motivation*. For example, foraging efficiency is usually a matter of trade-off among competing priorities. These may include energy gained versus energy spent, energy gained versus risk of predation, and energy gained versus losses to rivals.

Transitivity of choice Choosing to put things in order, or (by inference) placing an item in an ordered array.

Ultra-sociality is an enhanced form of social organization formed by cultural group-selection in humans, and by haplodiploidy in certain social insects.

Utility A term used in economics to denote the quantity maximized by the individual in the process of rational decision-making. In human microeconomics, utility is a notional measure of the psychological value of the consequences of an action (e.g. buying goods). It is notional, because we do not know how utility is incorporated into the decision-making process, only that animals behave as if they were maximizing some quantity, called utility. The evidence that animals behave in this way comes primarily from studies of transitivity of choice and of demand functions in animals. The concept of utility is important in the study of animal welfare and utility is sometimes seen as synonymous with welfare.

Wage rate The rate of return (in terms of energy, money, etc.) from working, foraging, and so on.

Notes

1 The Evolution of Economic Behaviour

1. Madeson, E.A., Tunney, R.J., Fieldman, G., Plotkin, H., Dunbar, R., Richardson, J., and McFarland, D. (2007) Kinship and altruism: a cross-cultural experimental study. *Brit. J. Psychol.*, 98, 339–359.
2. Fisher, R.A. (1930) *The Genetical Theory of Natural Selection.* Oxford University Press, Oxford; Haldane, J.B.S. (1955) Population genetics. *New. Biol.*, 18, 34–51; Hamilton, W.D. (1964) The general theory of social behaviour (I and II). *J. Theoret. Biol.*, 7, 1–16 and 17–32.
3. Packer, C. (1977) Reciprocal altruism in Papio Anubis. *Nature*, 265, 441–443.
4. Trivers, R. (1971) The evolution of reciprocal altruism. *Quart. Rev. Biol.*, 46, 35–57.
5. Marlar, P. and Mundinger, P. (1971) Vocal learning in birds. In Moltz, H. (ed) *The Ontogeny of Vertebrate Behaviour.* Academic Press, New York, NY.
6. Schmidt-Koenig, K. (1979) *Avian Orientation and Navigation.* Academic Press, London.
7. Davis, J.M. (1973) Imitation: a review and critique. In Bateson, P. and Klopfer, P. (eds) *Perspectives in Ethology.* Plenum Press, New York, NY; Rozin, P. (1976) The evolution of intelligence and access to the cognitive unconscious. *Prog. Physiol. Psychol.*, 6, 245–276; Bonner, J.T. (1983) *The Evolution of Culture in Animals.* Princeton University Press, Princeton, NJ.
8. Hinde, R. and Fisher, J. (1951) Further observations on the opening of milk bottles by birds. *Brit. Birds*, 44, 393–396.
9. Lawick-Goodall, J. van (1970) Tool-using in primates and other vertebrates. In Lehrman, D., Rosenblatt, J., Hinde, R. and Shaw, E. (eds) *Advances in the Study of Behavior.* Academic Press, New York, NY.
10. Eible-Eibesfeldt, I. (1967) Concepts of ethology and their significance in the study of human behaviour. In Stevenson, H. (ed) *Early Behaviour: Comparative and Developmental Approaches.* Wiley, New York.
11. Kortland, A. and Kooji, M. (1963) Protohominid behaviour in primates. *Symp. Zool. Soc. Lond.*, 10, 61–88; McGrew, W. (1975) Patterns of plant food sharing by wild chimpanzees. In Kawai, M., Kondo, S. and Ehara, A. (eds) *Contemporary Primatology: Proceedings of the Fifth Congress of the International Primatology Society*, S. Karger, Basel; McGrew, W.C., Tutin, C. and Baldwin, P. (1979) Chimpanzees, tools and termites: cross-cultural comparison of Senegal, Tanzania and Rio Muni. *Man*, 14, 185–214.
12. Kawamura, S. (1963) The process of sub-culture propagation among Japanese macaques. In Southwick, C. (ed) *Primate Social Behaviour.* Van Nostrand, New York, NY, pp. 82–90.

13. Lee, R.B. and Daly, R. (eds) (1999) *The Cambridge Encyclopedia of Hunters and Gatherers*. Cambridge University Press, Cambridge.
14. Frost, P. 2006. European hair and eye color: a case of frequency-dependent sexual selection? *Evol. Hum. Behav.*, 27, 85–103; Abbie, A.A. and Adey, W.R. (1953) Pigmentation in a central Australian tribe with special reference to fair-headedness. *Am. J. of Phys. Anthropol.*, 11, 339–359.
15. Ford, L., Graham, V., Wall, A., and Berg, J. (November, 2006) Vitamin D concentrations in an UK inner-city multicultural outpatient population. *Ann. Clin. Biochem.*, 43(6), 468–473; Signorello, L.B., Williams, S.M., Zheng, W., Smith, J.R., Long, J., Cai, Q., Hargreaves, M.K., Hollis. B.W., and Blot, W.J. (2010) Blood vitamin D levels in relation to genetic estimation of African ancestry. *Cancer Epidemiol. Biomark. Prev.*, 19(9), 2325–2331.
16. In 1871 Darwin published *The Descent of Man*, in which he considered the subject of sexual selection, to which he had referred to in his *The Origin of Species* (1859). According to Darwin, sexual selection depends upon the advantage which certain individuals have over others of the same sex and species solely in respect of reproduction. Darwin reasoned that females make a definite choice of sexual partner and that males have acquired particular adornments and courtship behaviour "not from being fitted to survive in the struggle for existence but from having gained an advantage over other males, and from having transmitted this advantage to their male offspring alone". Sexual selection is a complex subject that biologists have been arguing about for decades. For a good account, see Cronin, H. (1991) *The Ant and the Peacock*. Cambridge University Press, Cambridge.
17. The origin of the founder mutation, relating to eye colour, probably occurred in the Black Sea region, where the great agriculture migration to the northern part of Europe took place in the Neolithic periods about 6,000–10,000 years ago. The high frequency of blue-eyed individuals in the Scandinavian and Baltic areas indicates a positive selection for this phenotype. Several theories have been suggested to explain the evolutionary selection for such pigmentation traits, including the effects of ultraviolet light, vitamin D, and sexual selection. For further information see Eiberg, H., Troelsen, J., Nielsen, M., Mikkelsen, A., Mengel-From, J., Kjaer, K.W., and Hansen, L. (2008) Blue eye color in humans may be caused by a perfectly associated founder mutation in a regulatory element located within the HERC2 gene inhibiting OCA2 expression. *Hum. Genet.*, 123, 177–187.
18. The enzyme lactase, also called beta-D-galactosidase, is synthesized if at least one of the two genes for it is present. Only when both gene expressions are affected is lactase enzyme synthesis reduced, which in turn reduces lactose digestion. Lactase persistence, allowing lactose digestion to proceed, is the dominant allele. Physiological lactose intolerance, therefore, is an autosomal recessive trait. Lactose is a water soluble molecule, and when milk is separated into curds and whey, it is found in the water whey and not in the fatty curds. So, because the butter making separates milk's water components from the fat components, lactose

will not be present in the butter. Cheeses vary in their lactose content, depending upon the method of cheese making, but traditionally made yogurt contains lactase enzyme produced by the bacterial cultures used to make the yogurt. So lactose intolerant people can usually digest yogurt.

The prevalence of lactose intolerance varies markedly amongst modern human populations, and is related to their ancestral genetic makeup. It is very low in people with Scandinavian ancestors, including the Dutch, the British, and White North Americans, and very high in people of Mongolian descent, including the Chinese, other Asians, and Native Americans. The evidence comes from calculations about the rate of evolutionary change. The rate of change of gene frequency induced by natural selection depends upon the relative fitness of the various genotypes. The difference between two genotypes of differing fitness can be used to calculate the coefficient of selection against the inferior genotype, and this can be used to calculate the rate of change of phenotype within a population. In the case of the genotypes involved in lactose tolerance in human adults such calculations indicate that the relevant genetic changes are entirely possible within the 10,000 year time frame. For a brief account see McFarland, D. (1999) *Animal Behaviour*, 3rd edn. Longman, London, pp. 59–61. For substantive accounts see Bodmer, W.F. and Cavalli-Sforza, L. (1976) *Genetics, Evolution and Man*, W.H. Freeman, San Francisco; Flatz, G. (1987) Genetics of lactose digestion in humans. *Adv. Hum. Genet.*, 16, 1–77; Swallow, D.M. (2000) Genetics of lactase persistence and lactose intolerance. *Ann. Rev. Genet.*, 37, 197–219.

19. Evolution acting through natural selection represents an ongoing interaction between a species' genome (genetic makeup) and its environment over the course of many generations. Genetic traits may be positively or negatively selected relative to their concordance or discordance with environmental selective pressures. When the environment remains relatively constant, stabilizing selection tends to maintain genetic traits that represent the optimal average for a population. When environmental conditions permanently change, evolutionary discordance arises between a species' genome and its environment, and stabilizing selection is replaced by directional selection, which changes the average population genome. Initially, when permanent environmental changes occur in a population, individuals bearing the previous average status quo genome experience evolutionary discordance. In the affected genotype, this evolutionary discordance may manifest itself phenotypically as disease, increased morbidity and mortality, and reduced reproductive success. Konnor, M. (2001) Evolution and our environment. *West. J. Med.*, 174, 360–361. Konnor, M. and Boyd Eaton, S. (2010) Paleolithic nutrition 25 years later. *Nutr. Clin. Pract.*, 10, 594–602; McFarland, D. (2010) *Death by Eating. The Evolution of Human Food.* Amazon Create Space.

20. Key references are: Voegtlin, W.L. (1975) *The Stone Age Diet: Based on In-Depth Studies of Human Ecology and the Diet of Man.* Vantage Press, New York; Eaton, S.B. and Konner, M. (1985) Paleolithic nutrition: a consideration of its nature and current implications. *N. Engl. J. Med.*, 312, 283–289; Eaton, S.B., Konner, M., and Shostak, M. (1988) Stone agers in

the fast lane: chronic degenerative diseases in evolutionary perspective. *Am. J. Med.*, 84, 739–749; Eaton, S. Boyd, Eaton, Stanley B. III, Konner, M.J. and Shostak, M. (1996) An evolutionary perspective enhances understanding of human nutritional requirements. *J. Nutr.*, 126, 1732–1740; Eaton S.B., Eaton S.B.I. and Konner, M.J. (1999) Paleolithic nutrition revisited. In Trevathan, W.R., Smith, E.O. and McKenna, J.J. (eds) *Evolutionary Medicine.* Oxford University Press, New York, NY, p. 313.

21.   Richardson, P.J. and Boyd, R. (2005) *Not by Genes Alone: How Culture Transformed Human Evolution.* University of Chicago Press, Chicago.

22.   Choi, C. and Brahic, C. (2009) Found: a pocket guide to prehistoric Spain. *New Sci.*, 203 (2720), 8–9; Utrilla, P. Mazo C., Sopena, M.C., Martínez-Bea, M. Domingo, R. (2009) A Palaeolithic map from 13,660 calBP: engraved stone blocks from the late Magdalenian in Abauntz Cave (Navarra, Spain). *J. Hum. Evol.*, 57 (2).

23.   Tallerman, M. and Gibson, K. (2012) *The Oxford Handbook of Language Evolution.* Oxford University Press, Oxford; Pinker, S. and Bloom, P. (1990) Natural language and natural selection. *Behav. and Brain Sci.*, 13, 707–784; Tomasello, M. (1996) The cultural roots of language. In Velichkovski, B.M. and D.M. Rumbaugh (eds), *Communicating Meaning: The Evolution and Development of Language.* Z.I.F. Erlbaum, Mahwah, NJ; Pika, S. and Mitani, J. (2006) Referential gestural communication in wild chimpanzees (*Pan troglogytes*). *Curr. Biol.*, 16; Dunbar, R. (1996) *Grooming, Gossip and the Evolution of Language.* Faber and Faber, London; Falk, D. (August, 2004). Prelinguistic evolution in early hominins: whence motherese? *Behav. Brain Sci.*, 27(4), 491–503; discussion 503–583. Steels, L. (2009) Is sociality a crucial prerequisite for the emergence of language? In Botha, Rudolf P. and Knight, Chris (eds) *The Prehistory of Language.* Oxford University Press, Oxford, New York.

24.   Wade, N. (19 October, 2007) Neanderthals had important speech gene, DNA evidence shows. *New York Times*; Lieberman, P. and Crelin, E.S. (1971) On the speech of Neanderthal man. *Ling. Inq.*, 2(2), 203–222; Arensburg B., Tillier A., Vandermeersch, B., Duday, H., Schepartz, L.A. and Rak, Y. (1989) A middle Palaeolithic human hyoid bone. *Nature*, 338(6218), 758–760; Schwartz, J. and Tattersall I. (2000) The human chin revisited: what is it, and who has it? *J. Hum. Evol.*, 38(3), 367–409; Bocquet-Appel, J.-P. and Alain Tuffreau, A. (2009) Technological responses of Neanderthals to macroclimatic variations (240,000–40,000 BP). *Hum. Biol.* (Wayne State University Press) 81(2/3, Special issue on demography and cultural macroevolution), 287–307. Pettitt, P. (2000) Odd man out: Neanderthals and modern humans. *Brit. Archeol.*, 51, 1357–4442.

25.   Childe, G. (1942) *What Happened in History*, Penguin, London, p. 43; Childe, G. (1958) *The Prehistory of European Society*, Penguin, London, p. 35.

26.   Good accounts of domestication are given by Ucko, P.J. and Dimbleby, G.W. (eds) (1969) *The Domestication and Exploitation of Plants and Animals.* Gerald Duckworth & Co., London; and Diamond, Jared (1998) *Guns, Germs and Steel.* Vintage, London; and especially in Zohary, D. and

Hopf, M. (1993) *Domestication of Plants in the Old World*. Clarendon Press, Oxford.
27. Archaeologist J.R. Harlan discovered this by trying it himself in the mid-1960s. See Tannahill, R. (1975) *Food in History*. Paladin, Frogmore, St Albans, Herts, pp. 36–54.
28. Diamond, Jared (1998) *Guns, Germs and Steel*. Vintage, London, pp. 362–363.
29. It may well be that the cultivation of rice in China and Japan preceded the cultivation of cereals in the rest of the world. For a review, see Yoshinori, Y. (ed) (2002) *The Origins of Pottery and Agriculture*. Roli Books Pvt. Ltd., New Delhi.
30. Good references are Nentwig, W. (2007) Human environmental impact in the Paleolithic and Neolithic. In Henke, W. and Tattersall, I. (eds) *Handbook of Paleoanthropology*. Springer, Berlin; and Williams, M. (2002) *Deforesting the Earth: From Prehistory to Global Crisis*. University of Chicago Press, Chicago.
31. For further information see Gavrilov, L.A. and Gavrilova, N.S. (1991) *The Biology of Life Span: A Quantitative Approach*. Harwood Academic Publisher, New York.
32. There were differences in the timing of the Neolithic revolution across regions, and these generated significant variations in the genetic composition of the contemporary human populations. Combined with skeletal evidence, a picture emerges of the lifestyle of Neolithic farmers. For further details see Cohen, M.N. (1989) *Health and the Rise of Civilization*. Yale University Press, New Haven. For the effect of the Neolithic revolution on the exposure and the vulnerability of humans to environmental hazards such as infectious diseases see Diamond, Jared (1998) *Guns, Germs and Steel*. Vintage, London; and Weisdorf, J.L. (2006) From foraging to farming: explaining the Neolithic revolution, *Discussion papers* 03–41, University of Copenhagen, Dept. Economics. 2006.
33. Studies by Richard Lee of the Kalahari !Kung living a hunter-gatherer existence (see Lee, R. (1979) *The !Kung San*. Cambridge University Press, Cambridge) show that women are severely encumbered by their children. The women provide about two-thirds of calorie income by foraging for plant foods. Mongongo nuts are their most important food source. These are in plentiful supply in the dry season, but are usually situated some six miles from suitable camp sites. The women make excursions to gather these nuts every few days, taking their children with them. The men take no part in plant gathering, but confine themselves to hunting. Lee shows that the weight carried by mothers on the excursions increases with the frequency of having babies, not only because there are more mouths to feed, but also because the small children have to be carried. Nick Blurton Jones and Richard Sibly (Blurton Jones, N. and Sibly, R. (1978) Testing adaptiveness of culturally determined behaviour: do Bushman women maximise their reproductive success by spacing births widely and foraging seldom? In Reynolds, V. and Blurton-Jones (eds) *Human Behaviour and*

Adaptation. Taylor and Francis, London) show that an average birth spacing of four years is optimal under the prevailing conditions. Thus the women maximize their reproductive success by spacing births widely and by foraging seldom.

No such limitation exists when people live in permanent settlements, and so, as a result of the Neolithic revolution, it became possible for women to have children more frequently. As the techniques of plant cultivation and animal husbandry became more refined, it was possible to feed larger groups of people from relatively small numbers of food sources, and still have food left over for storage during the winter months. The ability to settle in one place, and to store food, led to a population explosion.

The human population 2,000 years ago was much larger than it was 10,000 years ago, so agricultural practices must have had a big impact on the environment in general, and on the lives of individuals in particular. In towns and villages, the population density was high, and the risk of cross-infection increased. Children of agriculturalists especially were more likely to die than were their hunter-gatherer counterparts. Land became enclosed for planting purposes, and people demanded property rights for the first time in history. This led to political developments, and there was much less equality than there had been in hunter-gatherer societies. A higher population density increases the level of technological sophistication, which in turn increases total productivity, allowing for further increases in population density. There comes a point where the environment reaches its carrying capacity.

In biological terms, the carrying capacity of the environment is the equilibrium population size of a species that can be supported by a region. In anthropology, it has been defined as the maximum human population that the region can support without progressive degradation. These definitions are somewhat simple, ignoring the possibility that there may be no static equilibrium, because the population can cycle or even vary chaotically. Moreover, the environment may be modified by the species to increase or reduce the population that it can support. In other words, the carrying capacity is partly a result of the environment itself, and partly a result of the behaviour of the inhabitants, both humans and other animals. For example, if goats are allowed to forage free and unrestricted, they soon exhaust their food supply, especially in dry areas. So an area of land that could support many goats turns into an area that can support fewer. Technological attempts to alter the carrying capacity of the environment can be a double-edged sword.

This is an area of active research by anthropologists, archaeologists, and economists. The following references provide an introduction: Cohen, Mark N. (1977) *The Food Crisis in Prehistory*. Yale University Press, New Haven; De Meza, David and Gould, J.R. (1992) The social efficiency of private decisions to enforce property rights. *J. Polit. Econ.*, 100, 561–580; Galor, Oded and Weil, D. (2000) Population, technology, and growth: from Malthusian stagnation to the demographic transition and beyond. *Am. Econ. Rev.*, 90, 806–828; Kremer, M. (1993) Population growth and technological change: one million BC to 1990. *Q. J. Econ.*, 108, 681–716; Galor, Oded and Weil, D. (1999) From Malthusian stagnation to modern growth. *Am. Econ. Rev.*, 89, 150–154; Pryor, Frederic L. (1986) The adoption of agriculture: some theoretical and empirical evidence. *Am. Anthropol.*, 88, 879–897; Pryor, Frederic L. (2004) From foraging to farming: the so-called "Neolithic revolution". *Res. Econ. Hist.*, 22, 1–41.

References to carrying capacity include Dewar, R.E. (1984) Environmental productivity, population regulation, and carrying capacity. *Am. Anthropol.*, 86(3), 601–614.; Moore, J. (1983) Carrying capacity, cycles and culture. *J. Hum. Evol.*, 12, 505–514. Zubrow, E.B.W. (1975). *Prehistoric Carrying Capacity: A Model.* Cummings Publishing Company, Menlo Park, CA.

34. Harris, M. (1985) Culture, People, Nature. 4th edn. Harper and Row, New York, NY, pp. 235–236.
35. For scientific evidence see Madsen, E.A., Tunney, R.J., Fieldman, G., Plotkin, H.C., Dunbar, R.I., Richardson, J.M., McFarland D. (2007) Kinship and altruism: a cross-cultural experimental study. *Brit. J. Psychol.*, 2007 May 98(Pt 2):, 339–359. For anthropological evidence, see Sahlins, M. (1974) *Stone Age Economics.* Tavistock Publications, London, pp. 196–204.
36. Quote is from Woodburn, J. (1968) An introduction to Hazda ecology. In Lee, R. and DeVore, I. (eds) *Man the Hunter.* Aldine, Chicago. Further discussion of this general point can be found in Sahlins, M. (1974) *Stone Age Economics.* Tavistock Publications, London, pp. 41–99.
37. Sahlins, M. (1974) *Stone Age Economics.* Tavistock Publications, London; the quote is from p. 37. Also Diamond, J. (1998) *Guns, Germs and Steel.* Vintage, London, pp. 265–292; the quote is from p. 176.
38. Ibid.
39. Ibid.
40. See note 33.
41. See note 35.
42. See note 36.
43. See note 27.

2   The Economic Behaviour of the Individual

1. Persky, Joseph. (1995) Retrospectives: the ethology of homo economicus. *J. Econ. Perspect.*, 9(2) (Spring), 221–231; Sen, A.K. (1977) Rational fools: a critique of the behavioural foundations of economic theory. *Phil. Pub. Aff.*, 317, 332. Sahlins, Marshall (1974) The original affluent society. In Sahlins, Marshall (ed) *Stone Age Economics.* Routledge, London. Polanyi, Karl (1944) *The Great Transformation.* Beacon Press, Boston. Mauss, Marcel (1924) *The Gift: The Form and Reason for Exchange in Archaic Societies.* Routledge, London.
2. Goss-Custard, J.D. (1977) Optimal foraging and size – selection of worms by redshank *Tringa totanus. Anim. Behav.*, 25, 10–29. Goss-Custard, J.D.

(1977) Predator responses and prey mortality in the redshank Tringa Totanus,(L) and a preferred prey *Corophium volutator* (Pallas). *J. Anim. Ecol.*, 46, 21–36.

3. Optimal foraging theory in its pure form asserts that animals forage in such a way as to maximize their net energy intake per unit time. Stephens, D. and Krebs, J. (1986) *Optimal Foraging Theory*. Princeton University Press, Princeton, NJ.

4. Tables 1 and 2 after Goss-Custard, J.D. (1977) Optimal foraging and size-selection of worms by redshank *Tringa totanus*. *Anim. Behav.*, 25, 10–29.

Table 1 Comparison of the Rates at which Redshank Obtained Energy in Three Sites Where They Mainly Took *Corophium* with the Rates They Would Have Achieved by Taking Worms Instead

Site	Rate of ingesting energy (cal min^{-1})	
	Potential rate from *Nereis* alone	Actual rate from mainly *Corophium*
9	234	88
10	224	70
11	185	93

Table 2 The Effort Expanded in Three Sites on Collecting 1 kcal by Birds Feeding Mainly on *Corophium* as They Actually Did, and on *Nereis* Alone

Site	Distance searched in metres		Number of pecks and probes made		Time spent swallowing prey (s)	
	Corophium	*Nereis*	*Corophium*	*Nereis*	*Corophium*	*Nereis*
9	103	42	470	165	62	48
10	150	44	671	167	121	49
11	106	56	543	198	79	48

5. Microeconomic theory can be applied to situations in which an actor has a choice among goods of different prices. The actor is assumed to be rational in the sense that transitivity of choice will be exhibited in relation to a complete set of goods; e.g. Edwards, W. (1954) The theory of decision making. *Psychol. Bull.*, 51, 380–417; Edwards, W. (1961)

Behavioural decision theory. *Ann. Rev. Psychol.*, 12, 473–498. However, rationality, in economic terms, is sometimes taken to relate to "a decision-making process that is based on making choices that result in the most optimal level of benefit or utility for the individual. Most conventional economic theories are created and used under the assumption that all individuals taking part in an action/activity are behaving rationally." Robson, A. (2001) The biological basis of economic behaviour. *J. Econ. Lit.*, XXXIX, pp. 11–33.

6. Some economists assume that rational decisions necessarily involve reasoning. However, people may make some decisions as a result of reasoning, but they may also make rational decisions in a purely automatic way, as if designed or programmed to do so. People also make irrational decisions. In fact, it is impossible to prove that human choices are transitive because to do so would involve repeated choice experiments under identical circumstances. This is not possible because circumstances are never exactly the same twice, if only because the memory of having made one choice changes the circumstances for the next (Edwards, W. (1961) Behavioural decision theory. *Ann. Rev. Psychol.*, 12, 473–498). Economists have to take transitivity of choice as a working hypothesis, an assumption upon which the elementary theory is based. There is, however, good experimental evidence that young children and monkeys do make transitive choices in behavioural tests, but that this ability probably does not involve reasoning (see note 14). Thus it may be that rational behaviour is a common feature of animal behaviour.

7. Ibid.

8. There is a considerable literature on transitivity of choice in animals. McGonigle, B. and Chalmers, M. (1992) Monkeys are rational. *Q. J. Exp. Psychol.*, 45(B), 198–228. Allen, C. (2006) Transitive inference in animals: reasoning or conditioned association? In Hurley, S. and Nudds, M. (eds) *Rational Animals*. Oxford University Press, Oxford. See also McFarland, D., Stenning, K. and McGonigle-Chalmers, M. (eds) (2012) *The Complex Mind: An Interdisciplinary Approach. Part I, Complexity and the Animal Mind.* Palgrave Macmillan, Basingstoke, 2012.

9. Transitivity of choice implies that something is maximized in the decision-making process. To see that this must be so, let us consider the following situation. Suppose A, B, and C can be evaluated numerically in some way. If A has a higher score than B, then we write $A > B$. A will be chosen over B by a person using a maximization principle (like choosing the option with the higher score). If we know that B has a higher score than C, we can write $B > C$. If C is chosen over A, it would appear that C has been allocated a higher score than A, but we know that $A > B > C$, which implies that C has a lower score than A. Thus, if C is chosen over A, C must be preferred even though it has a lower score than A. A person making choices on this intransitive basis could not be choosing the option with the largest number of points; such a person could not be using a maximization principle. If a person's preferences are

transitive, however, then we can deduce that he or she is using a maximizing principle, although the person may not be aware of it. For an extended discussion of animal rationality, see Bateson, M. (2010) Rational choice behavior: definitions and evidence. In Breed, M. and Moore, J. (eds). *Encyclopedia of Animal Behavior*, vol. 3. Academic Press, Oxford, pp. 13–19.

10. The equivalent of utility in some studies of animal behaviour is benefit (negative cost). Just as utility is a notional measure of the value of behaviour, so cost is a notional measure of the change in fitness that is associated with an animal's behaviour and its internal state. We do not know whether or not cost enters directly into the decision-making processes of animals. We can only test the hypothesis that animals behave in a way that maximizes benefit (minimizes cost). The components of cost include factors associated with the behaviour occurring at a particular time and risks associated with the animal's internal state. For example, an incubating gull incurs physiological cost in keeping the eggs warm, and it incurs costs as a result of its increasing hunger while on the nest. The various costs can be combined to form a *cost function*, which evaluates every aspect of the animal's state and behaviour in terms of its associated cost. In economics, the equivalent (but inverse) function is called a *utility function*. See McFarland, D. and Bosser, T. (1993) Intelligent Behavior in Animals and Robots. MIT Press, Cambridge, MA. See also McFarland, D. and Houston, A. (1981), *Quantitative Ethology: The State Space Approach*. Pitman, London.
11. Heinrich, B. (1979) *Bumblebee Economics*. Harvard University Press, Cambridge, MA.
12. Ibid.
13. Ibid.
14. Animals do not change their behaviour until they have accounted for the cost of changing. See Larkin, S. and McFarland, D. (1978) The cost of changing from one activity to another. *Anim. Behav.*, 26. 1237–1246. They found that the patterns of feeding and drinking in doves were altered in a predictable manner when the cost of changing from one to the other was increased in terms of time or of energy expenditure required. See also McFarland, D. (1989) *Problems of Animal Behaviour*. Longman, London.
15. Ibid.
16. Ibid.
17. Houston, A.I. and McFarland, D. (1980) Behavioural resilience and its relation to demand functions. In Staddon, J. (ed) *Limits to Action: The Allocation of Individual Behavior*. Academic Press, New York, NY, pp. 177–203.
18. Ibid.
19. For an account see McFarland, D. (1999) *Animal Behaviour*, 3rd edn. Pearson, London, p. 447.
20. Ibid.
21. McFarland, D. and Houston, A. (1981) *Quantitative Ethology: The State Space Approach*. Pitman, London; McFarland, D. (1989) *Problems of Animal Behaviour*. Longman, London.

22. See note 17.
23. Lea, S. and Roper, T. (1977) Demand for food on fixed ratio schedules as a function of the quality of concurrently available reinforcement. *J. Exp, Anal, Behav.*, 27, 371–380. See also Kagel, J.H., Battalio, R.C., Green, L. and Rachlin, H. (1980). Consumer demand theory applied to choice behavior of rats. In Staddon, J. (ed) *Limits to Action* Academic Press, New York, NY.
24. McFarland, D. (2012) *The Biology of Time*. Casacantarilla Publications, Amazon.
25. Lee, R.B. (1979) *The !Kung San. Men, Women and Work in a Foraging Society*. Cambridge University Press, Cambridge.
26. McFarland, D. (1989) Economic altruism. In McFarland, D. (ed) *Problems of Animal Behaviour*. Longman, London.
27. Ibid.
28. Ibid.
29. Allison, J. (1979) Demand economics and experimental psychology. *Behav. Sci.*, 24, 403–405. Allison, J. (1983) Behavioral substitutes and complements. In Melgren, R. (ed) *Animal Cognition and Behavior*. North Holland, Amsterdam; Lea, S. (1978) The psychology and economics of demand. *Psychol. Bull.*, 85, 441–466; Rachlin, H. (1980) Economics and behavioural psychology. In Staddon, J. (ed) *Limits to Action*. Academic Press, New York, NY.
30. See note 25.
31. See note 26.
32. See note 29.
33. Graeber, D. (2011) *Debt: The First 5000 Years*. Melville House Publishing, Brooklyn NY.
34. Bouman, John (2011) *Principles of Microeconomics*. Columbia, MD; Colander, David (2008) *Microeconomics*, 7th edn. McGraw-Hill; Pindyck, Robert S. and Rubinfeld, Daniel L. (2008) *Microeconomics*, 7th edn. Prentice Hall, Upper Saddle River, NJ.
35. Animals typically eat the most profitable prey types more than would be expected by chance since they appear in the diet at a higher proportion than they are encountered in the environment. Predators do not, however, eat only the most profitable prey types. Other prey types may be easier to find, and energy is not the only nutritional requirement. Toxins may be present in many prey types, therefore variability of diet prevents any one toxin from reaching dangerous levels. There are also other essential nutrients in all organism's diets, so it is clear that an approach focusing only on energy intake will not provide an adequate model. Davies, N.B., Krebs, J.R. and West, S.A. (2012) *An Introduction to Behavioral Ecology*. Wiley-Blackwell, West Sussex, UK.
36. McFarland, D. and Sibly, R. (1972) Unitary drives revisited. *Anim. Behav.*, 20, 548–563; Sibly, R. and McFarland, D. (1974) A state-space approach to motivation. In McFarland, D. (ed) *Motivational Control Systems Analysis*. Academic Press, London, pp. 213–250.
37. McFarland, D. and Bosser, T. (1993) *Intelligent Behaviour in Animals and Robots*. MIT Press, Cambridge, MA.

38. Simpson, S.J. and Raubenheimer, D. (1993) A multi-level analysis of feeding behaviour: the geometry of nutritional decisions. *Philos. Trans. R. Soc. Lond. B. Biol. Sci.*, 342, 381–402; Simpson, S. and Raubenheimer, D. (2012) *The Nature of Nutrition*. Princeton University Press, Princeton, NJ.
39. Ibid.
40. See note 36.
41. Spier, E. and McFarland, D. (1998) Learning to do without cognition. In R. Pfeifer Blamberg, B., Meyer, J. and Wilson, S. (eds) *Animals and Animats*. MIT Press, Cambridge, MA, pp. 38–47.
42. See note 38.
43. Rozin, P. (1967) Specific aversions as a component of specific hungers. *J. Comp. Physiol. Psychol.*, 64, 237–242; Rozin, P. and Kalat, J. (1971) Specific hungers and poison avoidance as adaptive specializations of learning. *Psychol. Rev.*, 78, 459–486.
44. For a fuller description see Graeber, D. (2011) *Debt: The First 5000 Years*. Melville House Publishing, Brooklyn, NY, Chapter 2.
45. The Finnish anthropologist Edvard Westermarck in his book (Westermarck, E. (1891) *The History of Human Marriage*. Macmillan, NY), suggested that there was a natural aversion to being sexually attracted to individuals that were playmates during the early years of life. Observations interpreted as evidence for the Westermarck effect have since been made in many places and cultures, including in the Israeli kibbutz system in which children were reared communally in peer groups, based on age, not biological relationships. It was discovered that out of the nearly 3,000 marriages that occurred across the kibbutz system, only 14 were between children from the same peer group. Of those 14, none had been reared together during the first six years of life. Shor, Eran and Simchai, Dalit (2009) Incest avoidance, the incest taboo, and social cohesion: revisiting Westermarck and the case of the Israeli kibbutzim. *Am. J. Sociol.* 114(6), 1803–1842; Lieberman, D., Tooby, J. and Cosmides, L. (2007) The architecture of human kin detection. *Nature*, 445, 727–731.

    Dual exogamy, in which both parties are the recipients of sexual favours, is found in various Australian, Turcic, African, Eskimo, and Finnic tribes. Such practices are basically cultural, but this does not mean that they have not been acted on by natural selection. Tribes in which there was too much inbreeding would suffer genetically, because the chances of offspring inheriting two copies of a defective gene would be high, with various deleterious consequences. (Such genetic principles apply to all species, not just humans.) Those societies that develop rituals that diminish inbreeding are more likely to survive in the long run. Thornhill, N. (1993) *The Natural History of Inbreeding and Outbreeding: Theoretical and Empirical Perspectives*. University of Chicago Press, Chicago, IL; Dorsten, L., Hotchkiss, L. and King, T. (1999) The effect of inbreeding on early childhood mortality: twelve generations of an Amish settlement. *Demography*, 36(2), 263–271.

3 Behavioural Economics

1. Ward Edwards is widely regarded as the founder of behavioural decision theory. His seminal papers are: Edwards, W. (1954) The theory of decision making. *Psychol. Bull.*, 41, 380–417; Edwards, W. (1961) Behavioral decision theory. *Annu. Rev. Psychol.*, 12, 473–498.
2. Kahneman, D. and Tversky, A. (1979) Prospect theory: an analysis of decision under risk. *Econometrica* (The Econometric Society), 47(2), 263–291
3. (a) Reference dependence: the decision-maker has a reference level when evaluating outcomes. The outcomes are then compared to the reference point and classified as gains(above) or losses (below) in relation to the reference point.
   (b) Loss aversion: losses carry more weight than equivalent gains.
   (c) Probability weighting: decision-makers give more weight to small probabilities than they do to large probabilities, resulting in an inverse S shaped probability weighting function.
   (d) Diminishing sensitivity to gains and losses: the decision-maker's satisfaction (utility) falls as the size of gains and losses (relative to the reference point) increases in absolute value.
4. Tversky, Amos and Kahneman, Daniel (1992) Advances in prospect theory: cumulative representation of uncertainty. *J. Risk Uncertainty*, 5(4), 297–323.
5. For details see note 3.
6. Battalio, Raymond, C. & Green, Leonard & Kagel, John, H. (1981) Income–leisure tradeoffs of animal workers. *Am. Econ. Rev.*, 71(4), 621–632; Kagel, J.H. and Battalio, R.C. (1981) Demand curves for animal consumers. *Q. J. Econ.*, 96(1), 1–16.
7. Kagel, J.H. et al. (1995) *Economic Choice Theory: An Experimental Analysis of Animal Behavior.* Cambridge University Press, New York; Rabin, Matthew (1998) Psychology and economics. *J. Econ. Lit.*, 36; Chen, M.K. Lakshminaryanan, V., & Santos, L. (2006) How basic are behavioral biases? Evidence from Capuchin monkey trading behavior. *J. Polit. Econ.*, 114(3), 517–537; Rubin, Paul H. and Monica Capra, C. (2011) The evolutionary psychology of economics. In Roberts, S. Craig (ed) *Applied Evolutionary Psychology.* Oxford University Press, Oxford; Aggarwal, Raj (2014) Animal spirits in financial economics: a review of deviations from economic rationality. *Int. Rev. Finan. Anal.*, 32(1), 179–187.
8. Ibid.
9. Moore, B.R. (1973) The role of directed Pavlovian reactions in simple instrumental learning in the pigeon. In Hinde, R.A. and Stevenson-Hinde, J. (eds) *Constraints on Learning.* Academic Press, London.
10. Brown, P.L. and Jenkins, H.M. (1968) Autoshaping of the pigeons key peck. *J. Exp. Anal. Behav.*, 11, 1–8.
11. Williams, D. and Williams, H. (1969) Auto-maintenance in the pigeon: sustained pecking despite contingent non-reinforcement. *J. Exp. Anal. Behav.*, 12, 511–520.

12. McFarland, D. (1974) Time-sharing as a behavioural phenomenon. In Lehrman, D., Rosenblatt, J., Hinde, R., and Shaw, E. (eds) *Advances in the Study of Behaviour*. Academic Press, New York.

13. Sibly, R. and McFarland, D. (1976) On the fitness of behaviour sequences. *Am. Nat.*, 110, 601–617.

14. Meddis, R. (1975) On the function of sleep. *Anim. Behav.*, 23, 676–691; Meddis, R. (1977) *The Sleep Instinct*. Routledge & Kegan Paul, London. McFarland, D. (1989) Sleep as an ethological problem. In McFarland, D. *Problems of Animal Behaviour*. Longman, London.

15. McFarland. D. (2012) *The Biology of Time*. Casacantarilla Publications, Lanzarote.

16. McFarland. D. (1989) Suffering in animals. In McFarland, D. (ed) *Problems of Animal Behaviour*. Longman, London.

17. Garner J.P. and Mason G.J. (2002) Evidence for a relationship between cage stereotypies and behavioural disinhibition in laboratory rodents. *Behav. Brain Res.*, 136(1), 83–92; Swaisgood, R. and Shepherdson, D.J. (2005) Scientific approaches to enrichment and stereotypies in zoo animals: what's been done and where should we go next?. *Zoo. Biol.*, 24(6), 499–518; Lawrence, A.B. and Terlouw, E.M. (1993) A review of behavioral factors involved in the development and continued performance of stereotypic behaviors in pigs. *J. Anim. Sci.*, 71(10), 2815–25.

18. Ibid.

19. Ibid.

20. For a discussion of the role of biological clocks in the real world, see McFarland, D. (2012) *The Biology of Time*. Casacantarilla Publications, Lanzarote; Nicholson, P.J. and D'Auria, D.A. (1999) Shift work, health, the working time regulations and health assessments. *Occup. Med. (Lond.)*, 49(3), 127–37; Knutsson, A., Åkerstedt, T., Jonsson, B., Orth-Gomer, K. (1986) Increased risk of ischaemic heart disease in shift workers. *Lancet*, 1986; 2: 89–92. Knutsson A. Shift work and coronary heart disease. Scand J Soc Med 1989; 44(Suppl.): 1–36.

21. Drent, R. (1970) Functional aspects of incubation in the herring gull. In *The Herring Gull and Its Egg*, Part 1. In Baerends, G. and Drent, R. (eds) *Behaviour*, 82, 1–132.

22. Sibly, R. and McCleery, R. (1985) Optimal decision rules for gulls. *Animal Behaviour*, 33, 449–465.

23. Ibid.

24. Goss-Custard, J.D. (1977) Optimal foraging and size-selection of worms by redshank *Tringa totanus*. *Anim. Behav.*, 25, 10–29; Goss-Custard, J.D. (1977) Predator responses and prey mortality in the redshank *Tringa Totanus*,(L) and a preferred prey *Corophium volutator* (Pallas). *J. Anim. Ecol.*, 46, 21–36; Barnard, C.J. (1984) *Producers and scroungers*. Chapman and Hall, London; McFarland, D. (1989) Economic altruism. In McFarland, D. (ed) *Problems of Animal Behaviour*. Longman, London; Gowdy, J. (ed) (1997) *Limited Wants, Unlimited Means: A Reader on Hunter-Gatherer Economics*. Island Press, Washington, DC.

25. Niebuhr, V. and McFarland, D. (1983) Nest-relief behaviour in the herring gull. *Anim. Behav.*, 31, 701–707.
26. Early studies of risk were primarily theoretical, e.g. Friedman, Milton and Savage, Leonard J. (1948) The utility analysis of choices involving risk. *Polit. Econ.*, 56, 279–304; Kami, Edi and Schmeidler, David (1986) Self-preservation as a foundation of rational behavior under risk. *Econ. Behav. Org.*, 7, 71–81; Rubin, Paul H. and Paul, Ghris W. (1979) An evolutionary model of taste for risk. *Econ. Inq.*, 17, 585–596. These were followed by animal-psychology experiments, e.g. Kagel, J.H. et al. (1981) Demand curves for animal consumers. *Q. J. Econ.*, 96(1), 1–16; Battalio, Raymond C, Kagel, John H. and MacDonald, Don N. (1985) Animals' choices over uncertain outcomes: some initial experimental results. *Am. Econ. Rev.*, 75, 596–613; Kagel, John H., Battalio, Raymond C. and Green, Leonard (1995) *Economic Choice Theory: An Experimental Analysis of Animal Behavior.* Cambridge University Press, Cambridge; Chen, M.K. et al. (2006) How basic are behavioral biases? Evidence from Capuchin monkey trading behavior. *J. Polit. Econ.*, 114(3), 517–537. More recently, there have been many biological studies in both laboratory and field, e.g. Reboreda, Juan C. and Kacelnik, Alex (1991) Risk sensitivity in starlings. *Behav. Ecol.*, 2, 301–309; Bateson, Melissa and Kacelnik, Alex (1996) Rate currencies and the foraging starling: the fallacy of the averages revisited. *Behav. Ecol.*, 7, 341–52. Kacelnik, Alex and Bateson, Melissa (1996) Risky theories: the effects of variance on foraging theories. *Am. Zool.*, 36, 402–434; Houston, A. (1997) Natural selection and context-dependent values. *Proc. Roy. Soc. Lond. B.*, 264, 1539–1541; Hurly, T. and Oseen, M. (1999) Context-dependent, risk-sensitive foraging preferences in wild rufous hummingbirds. *Anim. Behav.*, 58, 59–65. Waite, T.A. (2001) Intransitive preferences in hoarding gray jays (*Perisoreus Canadensis*). *Behav. Ecol. and Sociobiol.*, 50, 116–121; Bateson, M. (2002) Context-dependent foraging choices in risk-sensitive starlings. *Anim. Behav.*, 64, 251–260; Bateson, M., Healy, S. and Hurly, T. (2002) Irrational choices in hummingbird foraging. *Anim. Behav.*, 63, 587–596; Schuck-Paim, C. and Kacelnic, A. (2002) Rationality in risk-sensitive foraging choices by starlings. *Anim. Behav.*, 64, 869–879; Schafir, S., Waite, T. and Smaith, B. (2002) Context-dependent violations of rational choice in honeybees (*Apis Melifera*) and grey jays (*Perisoreus Canadensis*). *Behav. Ecol. and Sociobiol.*, 51, 180–187. These biological studies show that risk sensitivity is widespread in the animal kingdom, and is often context dependent.
27. Ibid.
28. Shernhammer, E., Laden, F., Speizer, F., Willett, W., Hunter, D., Kawachi, I., and Colditz, G. (2001) Rotating night shifts and risk of breast cancer in women participating in the nurses' health study. *J. Natl. Cancer Inst.*, 93, 1563–81; Knutsen, A. et al. (1986) Increasing risk of ischaemic heart disease in shift workers. *Lancet*, 2(8498), 89–92.
29. Ibid.
30. For a discussion, see McFarland, D. (2012) *The Biology of Time.* Casacantarilla Publications, Lanzarote. Bailey, R.C. and Devore, I. (1989)

Research on the Efe and Lese populations of the Ituri forest, Zaire. *Am. J. Phys. Anthropol.*, 78, 459–471.

31. Cook, Earl (1971) The flow of energy in an industrial society. *Sci. Am.*, 225, 135–144. For a discussion see Morris, I. (2011) *Why the West Rules – For Now.* Profile Books, London, pp. 153–157. The adoption of agriculture was a transformation that can be understood as a leap to ultra-sociality. This is a type of social organization that is evident in some species of ants and termites; it enables them to greatly increase their energy production. The suggestion is "that the origin of human and insect agriculture is an example of parallel evolution driven by similar forces of multi-level selection". Gowdy, J. and Krall, L. (2013) Ultrasociality and the origin of the Anthropocene. *Ecol. Econ.*, 95, 137–147; Gowdy, J. and Krall, L. (2014) Agriculture and the evolution of human ultrasociality. *J. Bioecon.*, 16(2), 179–202.

32. Ibid.

33. McFarland, D. and Houston, A. (1981) *Quantitative Ethology: The State Space Approach.* (Appendix 7). Pitman Books, London. McFarland, D. and Bosser, T. (1993) *Intelligent Behaviour in Animals and Robots.* MIT Press, Cambridge, MA.

34. There is a considerable literature on animal hoarding, stretching over the past 35 years. The references below, in chronological order, give some indication of the sophistication of animal hoarding, and of our understanding of it. Stapanian, M.A. and Smith, C.C. (1984) Density-dependent survival of scatterhoarded nuts: an experimental approach. *Ecology*, 65, 1387–1396; Clarkson, K., Eden, S.F., Sutherland, W.J. and Houston, A.I. (1986) Density, dependence and magpie hoarding. *J. Anim. Ecol.*, 55, 111–121; Vander Wall, Stephen B. (1990) *Food Hoarding in Animals.* University of Chicago Press, Chicago; Emery, N.J. and Clayton, N.S. (2001) Effects of experience and social context on prospective caching strategies by scrub jays. *Nature*, 414, 443–446; Bugnyarf, T. and Kotrschal, K. (2002) Observational learning and the raiding of food caches in ravens, *Corvus corax*: is it "tactical" deception? *Anim. Behav.*, 64, 185–195; Vander Wall, S.B. and Jenkins, S.H. (2003) Reciprocal pilferage and the evolution of food-hoarding behavior. *Behav. Ecol.*, 14(5); Dally, Joanna M., Emery, Nathan J. and Clayton, Nicola S. (2006) Food-caching western scrub-jays keep track of who was watching when. *Science*, 312(5780), 1662–1665.

35. Testart, A. (1982) The significance of food storage among hunter-gatherers: residence patterns, population densities, and social regularities. *Curr. Anthropol.*, 23(5); Kaplan, H. and Hill, K. (1985) Food sharing among cache foragers: tests of explanatory hypotheses. *Curr. Anthropol.*, 26, 223–245; Douglas, B. and Ray, D. (1987) Economic growth with intergenerational altruism. *Rev. Econ. Stud.*, 54, 227–241; Kaplan, H. and Hill, K. (1992) The evolutionary ecology of food acquisition. In Smith, E. and Winterhalder, B. (eds) *Evolutionary Ecology and Human Behavior.* Aldine de Gruyter, New York, NY, 167–201; Noe, R., Van Hoof, J. and Hammerstein, P. (eds) (2006) *Economics in Nature: Social Dilemmas, Mate Choice and Biological Markets.* Cambridge University Press, Cambridge, MA; Rubin, Paul

H. and Monica Capra, C. (2011) The evolutionary psychology of economics. In Roberts, S. Craig (ed) *Applied Evolutionary Psychology*. Oxford University Press, Oxford.

36. In mammals, excess food energy is stored as fat in subcutaneous and abdominal depots. The dominant fatty acids in the fat storage depots of wild mammals are saturated fatty acids, whereas the dominant fatty acids in muscle and all other organ tissues are poly-unsaturated fatty acids and mono-unsaturated fatty acids. Because subcutaneous and abdominal body fat stores are depleted during most of the year in wild animals, most of the total carcass fat is of the poly- and mono-unsaturated type. A year-round dietary intake of high amounts of saturated fatty acids would have not been possible for pre-agricultural humans preying on wild mammals, whereas when a domesticated animal is slaughtered for food, everything is eaten, including the storage fat, which contains large amounts of saturated fatty acids. For further details see Cordain, L., Watkins, B.A., Florant, G.L., Kehler, M., Rogers, L., and Li, Y. (2002) Fatty acid analysis of wild ruminant tissues: evolutionary implications for reducing diet-related chronic disease. *Eur. J. Clin. Nutr.*, 56, 181–891.

37. Frost, R. and Hartl, T. (1996) A cognitive-behavioral model of compulsive hoarding. *Behav. Res. Ther.*, 34(4), 341–350; Steketee, G., Frost, R. (December, 2003) Compulsive hoarding: current status of the research. *Clin. Psychol. Rev.*, 23(7), 905–927; Tolin, David F., Meunier, Suzanne A., Frost, Randy O., and Steketee, Gail (2010) Course of compulsive hoarding and its relationship to life events. *Depress. Anxiety*, 27, 829–838; Pertusa, A., Frost, R.O., Fullana, M. A., Samuels, J., Steketee, G., Tolin, D., Saxena, S., Leckman, J.F., and Mataix-Cols, D. (2010) Refining the boundaries of compulsive hoarding: a review. *Clin. Psychol. Rev.*, 30, 371–386.

38. Ibid.

39. Ibid.

40. Dreske, F. (1988) *Explaining Behaviour: Reasons in a World of Causes*. MIT Press, Cambridge, MA; Dreske, F. (2006) Minimal rationality. In Hurley, S. and Nudds, M. (eds) *Rational Animals*. Oxford University Press, Oxford.

41. Allen, C. (2006) Transitivity in animals: reasoning or conditioned associations? In Hurley, S. and Nudds, M. (eds) *Rational Animals*. Oxford University Press, Oxford. See also chapters 1, 2, 4, and 5 in McFarland, D., Stenning, K. and McGonigle-Chalmers, M. (eds) (2012) *The Complex Mind: An Interdisciplinary Approach*. Palgrave Macmillan, Basingstoke.

42. Ibid.

43. Samuelson, P.A. (1976) *Economics*, 10th edn. McGraw-Hill, New York, NY.

44. McFarland, D.J. (1971) *Feedback Mechanisms in Animal Behaviour*. Academic Press, London, pp. 279; McFarland, D.J. and Houston, A. (1981) *Quantitative Ethology: The State Space Approach*. Pitman Books, London, pp. 204.

45. Grafen, A. (1999) Formal Darwinism, the individual-as-maximising-agent analogy, and bet-hedging. *Proc. R. Soc. Lond., Ser. B*, 266, 799–803; Hurley, S. and Nudds, M. (eds) (2006) *Rational Animals*. Oxford University Press, Oxford; Bateson, M. (2010) Rational choice behaviour: definitions and

evidence. In Breed, M.D. and Moore, J. (eds) *Encyclopedia of Animal Behavior*, vol. 3, Academic Press, Oxford, pp. 13–19.

46. Kacelnic, A. (2006) Meanings of rationality. In Hurley, S. and Nudds, M. (eds) *Rational Animals*, Oxford University Press, Oxford.
47. Ibid.
48. Hurly, T. and Oseen, M. (1999) Context-dependent, risk-sensitive foraging preferences in wild rufous hummingbirds. *Anim. Behav.*, 58, 59–65; Bateson, M., Healy, S. and Hurly, T. (2002) Irrational choices in hummingbird foraging. *Anim. Behav.*, 63, 587–596.
49. Ibid.
50. Ibid.
51. See note 46.
52. Kalencher, T. and Winterden, M. (2011) Why we should use animals to study economic decision making – a perspective. *Front. Neurosci.*, 5, 82.

4   The Biological Bases of Decision-Making

1. Allen, C. (2006) Transitive inference in animals: reasoning or conditioned associations. In Hurley, S. and Nudds, M. (eds) *Rational Animals*. Oxford University Press, Oxford; McGonigle, B. and Chalmers, M. (1986) Representations and strategies during inference. In Myers, T., Brown, K., & McGonigle, B. (1986). *Reasoning and Discourse Processes*, Academic Press, London.
2. Ibid.
3. Zach, R. (1979) Shell dropping: decision making and optimal foraging in northwestern crows. *Behaviour*, 68, 106–117.
4. Sibly, R. (1983) Optimal group size is unstable. *Anim. Behav.*, 31, 947–948.
5. McFarland, D. (1974) Time-sharing as a behavioural phenomenon. In Lehrman, D., Rosenblatt, J., Hinde, R. and Shaw, E. (eds) *Advances in the Study of Behavior*. Academic Press, New York, NY; Sibly, R. and McFarland, D. (1976) On the fitness of behaviour sequences. *Am. Nat.*, 110, 601–617; McFarland, D. and Houston, A. (1981) *Quantitative Ethology: The State-Space Approach*. Pitman Books, London; Milinski, M. and Heller, R. (1978) Influence of a predator on the optimal foraging behaviour of sticklebacks (*Gastterosteus aculeatus* L). *Nature, London*, 275, 642–644; McCleery, R. (1978) Optimal behaviour sequences and decision-making. In Krebs, J. and Davies, N. *Behavioural Ecology*. Blackwell Scientific Publications, Oxford.
6. Ibid.
7. Ibid.
8. Ibid.
9. Cabanac's work on humans includes: Cabanac, M. (1986) Performance and perception of various combinations of treadmill speed and slope. *Physiol. Behav.*, 38, 839–843; Cabanac, M. and Leblanc, J. (1983) Physiological conflict in humans: fatigue vs cold discomfort. *Am. J. Physiol.*, 244, 621–628; Cabanac, M. (1995) Palatability versus money: experimental study of conflict motivations. *Appetite*, 25, 43–49; Cabanac,

M. (1986) Money versus pain: experimental study of conflict in humans. *J. Exp. Anal. Behav.*, 46, 37–44; Johnson, K. and Cabanac, M. (1981). Human thermoregulatory behaviour during a conflict between cold discomfort and money. *Physiol. Behav.*, 30, 145–150.
10. Ibid.
11. Ibid.
12. Ibid.
13. Ibid.
14. Ibid.
15. Ibid.; Cabanac, M. (1992) Pleasure: The common currency. *J. Theor. Biol.*,155, 173–200.
16. McFarland, D. (1989) Goal-directed behaviour. In McFarland, D. (ed) *Problems of Animal Behavior*. Longman, London. See McFarland, D. (1999) *Animal Behaviour, Psychobiology, Ethology and Evolution*, 3rd edn. Pearson Education, Harlow, UK. Chapter 24 for a review of this area. See also Cuthill, J. and Houston, A. (1997) Managing time and energy. In Krebs, J. and Davies, N. (eds) *Behavioural Ecology*, 4th edn. Blackwell, Oxford.
17. Ibid.
18. These issues are discussed in Montefiore, A. and Noble, D. (eds) (1989) *Goals, No Goals and Own Goals*. Unwin Hyman, London; and in Kennedy, J. (1992) *The New Anthropomorphism*. Cambridge University Press, Cambridge.
19. Ibid.
20. Nisbett, Richard E. and Wilson, Timothy D. (1977) Telling more than we can know: verbal reports on mental processes. *Psychol. Rev.* 84, 231–259, reprinted in Lewis Hamilton, David (ed) (2005) *Social Cognition: Key Readings*. Psychology Press, New York and Brighton/Hove; Wilson, Timothy D. and Dunn, Elizabeth W. (2004) Self-knowledge: its limits, value, and potential for improvement. *Annu. Rev. Psychol.*, 55(1), 507; Pronin, Emily (2009) The introspection illusion. In Zanna, Mark P. (eds) *Advances in Experimental Social Psychology*, vol. 41, Academic Press, Waltham, MA, pp. 52–53; Cabanac (1992) Pleasure, 173–200.
21. Ibid.
22. Ibid.
23. Cabanac, M. (1986) Money versus pain: experimental study of conflict in humans. *J. Exp. Anal. Behav.*, 46, 37–44.
24. Animal intentionality, if it exists, would probably not include the whole panoply of mental states, but it would have to include some aspect of aboutness.
25. For discussion of this view, see Montefiore, M. and Noble, D. (1989) *Goals, No-Goals and Own Goals: A Debate on Goal-Directed and Intentional Behaviour*. Unwin Hyman, London. See also McFarland, D. (1989) *Problems of Animal Behaviour*. Longman, London, Chapter 5.
26. See Kennedy, J. (1992) *The New Anthropomorphism*; and McFarland, D. (2008) *Guilty Robots, Happy Dogs. The Question of Alien Minds*. Oxford University Press, Oxford, pp. 161–163.
27. Ibid.

28. Ibid.
29. For discussion of this view, see Montefiore, M. and Noble, D. (1989) *Goals, No-Goals and Own Goals: A Debate on Goal-directed and Intentional Behaviour.* Unwin Hyman, London. See also McFarland, D. (1989) *Problems of Animal Behaviour,* Chapter 5, and Kennedy, J. (1992) *The New Anthropomorphism.* For a more philosophical discussion see McFarland, D. (2008) *Guilty Robots, Happy Dogs,* pp. 161–163.
30. Ibid.
31. Ibid.
32. See Montefiore and Noble (1989) *Goals, No-Goals and Own Goals,* p 211 onwards.
33. Trivers, R. (1985) *Social Evolution.* Benjamin-Cummings, Menlo Park, CA. See also Trivers, R. (2014) *The Folly of Fools: The Logic of Deceit and Self-Deception in Human Life.* Basic Books, New York; Hagen, E., Chater, N., Gallistell, C., Houston, A., Kacelnic, A., Kalencher, T., Nettle, D., Oppenheimer, D., and Stephens, D. (2012) What can evolution do for us? In Hammerstein, P. and Stevens, J. (eds) *Evolution and the Mechanisms of Decision Making. Strungmann Forum* (J. Lupp series editor). Report 11. MIT Press, London. See also Richardson, P.J. and Boyd, R. (2005) *Not by Genes Alone: How Culture Transformed Human Evolution.* University of Chicago Press, Chicago.
34. Ibid.
35. Elworthy, C. (1993) *Homo Biologicus: An Evolutionary Model for the Human Sciences.* Dunker and Humblot, Berlin.
36. Ibid.
37. Dohmen, T., Falk, A., Huffman, D., and Sunde, U. (2009) Homo reciprocans: survey evidence on behavioural outcomes. *Econ. J.,* 119(536), 592; Persky, Joseph. (1995) Retrospectives: the ethology of homo economicus. *J. Econ. Perspect.,* 9(2), (Spring, 1995), 221–231.
38. Ibid.
39. Ibid.

Index

CPI Antony Rowe
Chippenham, UK
2016-12-23 21:23